The Descendants of
Anton Vogelbach
and Elisabeth Schneebeli

Vogelbach Family Stories

Catherine Doheny Dente

Decorative font used throughout book is called Imprint MT Shadow

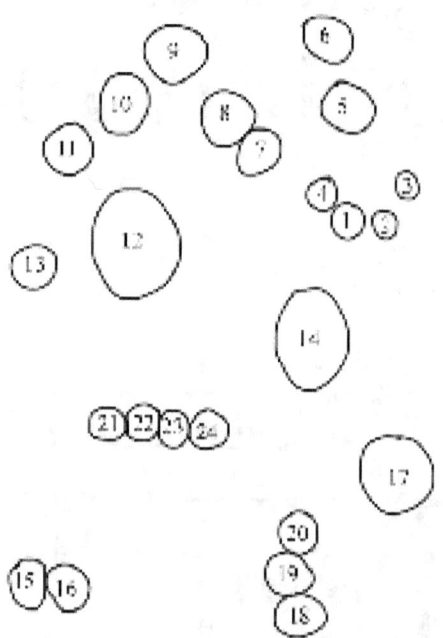

Key to Cover photos:

1. Anton Vogelbach
2. Mary Vogelbach
3. Son of Anton
4. Son of Anton
5. Otto Vogelbach
6. Louis Vogelbach
7. Adolph Vogelbach
8. Fanny Moritz
9. Olga Vogelbach
10. John Vogelbach
11. Martha Vogelbach
12. Adolph Vogelbach
13. Barbara Hassler
14. John Vogelbach
15. John Vogelbach
16. Fanny Moritz
17. Joseph Vogelbach
18. Virginia Vogelbach
19. Joan Vogelbach
20. Grace Vogelbach
21. Grace Vogelbach
22. Virginia Vogelbach
23. Jean Vogelbach
24. Joan Vogelbach

ISBN 1442106670

EAN-13   9781442106673

Printed in the United States of America by CreateSpace,
a DBA of On-Demand Publishing LLC, part of the Amazon group of companies.

Acknowledgements

Thank you to the many, many cousins who shared names and dates of their family members' births, marriages, and deaths.

Special thanks go to my mother Grace (Vogelbach) Doheny, my sister Elizabeth (Doheny) Gundlach, Aunt Joan (Vogelbach) Martin, Aunt Virginia (Vogelbach) Black, my cousins Veronica Black, John Black, Ruth (Ritter) Bush, Olga (Jargstorff) Hughes, Charles Roebuck, and Peter Heidtmann for sharing many family stories and photographs with me.

Thank you for the warm encouragement of so many other cousins during this project.

I am indebted to Judy Hall, a member of my wonderful book club, for helping me with Chapter Four and to my cousin Charles Roebuck who gave me invaluable stylistic suggestions throughout the book.

This family research has given me the pleasure of re-establishing ties with many first cousins and of beginning new friendships with several second and third cousins.

What a joy!

Catherine (Doheny) Dente

Our European Origins

Map adapted by the author from free outline map at http://maps.unomaha.edu by Dr. David Peterson.

1 – SAXONY	Beyer and Müller families
2 – BADEN in SW Germany	Rapp and Wagner families
3 – ZÜRICH, Switzerland, and nearby towns	Vogelbach and Moritz families
4 – ALSACE, France	Moritz family

The author has written books about each of these families.

Contents

Table of Illustrations

A Word about the
Genealogical Numbering System

Genealogical Summaries appear at the end of each chapter. Numbers are assigned to the people covered in the genealogy. The numbering system employed in this book is called the Modified Register System. It is based on the numbering system devised by the *New England Historic and Genealogical Register Quarterly* (NGQ) and later refined by the *National Genealogical Society Quarterly* (NGSQ). In this numbering system, everyone in a direct line from progenitor (oldest U.S.A. immigrant ancestor) on down gets a unique Arabic number to the left of their name. The progenitor's male parent is assigned a capital letter, which denotes an ancestor of foreign birth. Women are numbered only if they are direct descendants of the progenitor. Names in the genealogy are in SMALL CAPS, and the first child's given name is followed by his or her New World generation number. Italicized names with superscripts appear in parentheses enabling you to trace parentage several generations back. Only the first child's name is followed by these parentheses, but the parentage applies to all of the siblings.

For example, Chapter Three mentions these children of John and Fanny Vogelbach:

> **17.** i. OTTO ANDREAS^2 VOGELBACH (*John^1, Anton^A*) was born 9 Nov 1887 in Manhattan, NY.
> + **18.** ii. JOSEPH ANTHONY VOGELBACH was born 23 Aug 1889 in Corona, Flushing, NY.

The bold numbers are Otto and Joseph's unique Arabic numbers in the system. *John^1* is the progenitor, and *Anton^A* is John's father who did not emigrate to the U.S.A. The italicized names *John^1* and *Anton^A* follow the name of just the oldest child OTTO ANDREAS. The plus sign (+) in front of JOSEPH indicates that more is known about him than what appears in the Genealogical Summary, and a succeeding chapter will contain more information.

A Letter to My Sisters, My Cousins, Their Children, and Their Grandchildren

Who were our Vogelbach ancestors? I've tried to answer that for myself and for you in this book. Hopefully, the stories I've included will make our ancestors real for you and keep a memory of them alive. All the usual genealogical statistics of birth dates, marriage dates, and death dates are on these pages, but you will also read about immigration, occupations, residences, our ancestors' religions, and some old family stories that have been passed down for the last one hundred thirty years.

I became fascinated by family history when I was about 25 and attended a reunion of my mother's cousins. A relative named Harold Helliesen displayed a family tree that he had drawn for the Helliesen side of his family. From that moment on, I dreamed about creating my own family tree, and I was determined to research my family history when I had the time. Genealogy became my favorite hobby after I retired in 1994.

My mother had told me that her parents were born in this country. She knew her father's parents were immigrants, but she wasn't sure about her mother's parents. I wondered, "Who were my ancestors? What made them leave Europe? What was the trans-Atlantic voyage like for them? What were their lives like when they came to America? How did they support their families? How many cousins did I have?" I set out on a grand hunt to find the answers to these questions and more.

All of my first cousins had been very close when we were children, and I was glad to have an excuse to talk with them again while I researched this book. I also met and corresponded with many second and third cousins from the various branches of my family tree. It has been a most enjoyable fourteen-year project.

Nothing on these pages is fiction. I've made a tremendous effort to document every fact in the book. When I have been forced to make a reasonable guess, I have indicated this to the reader. There are many, many footnotes, and you may certainly ignore them and simply enjoy the narrative, but the sources are there for anyone who is interested in knowing where my information came from.

Catherine (Doheny) Dente

Vogelbach Residences
1880s to 1930s

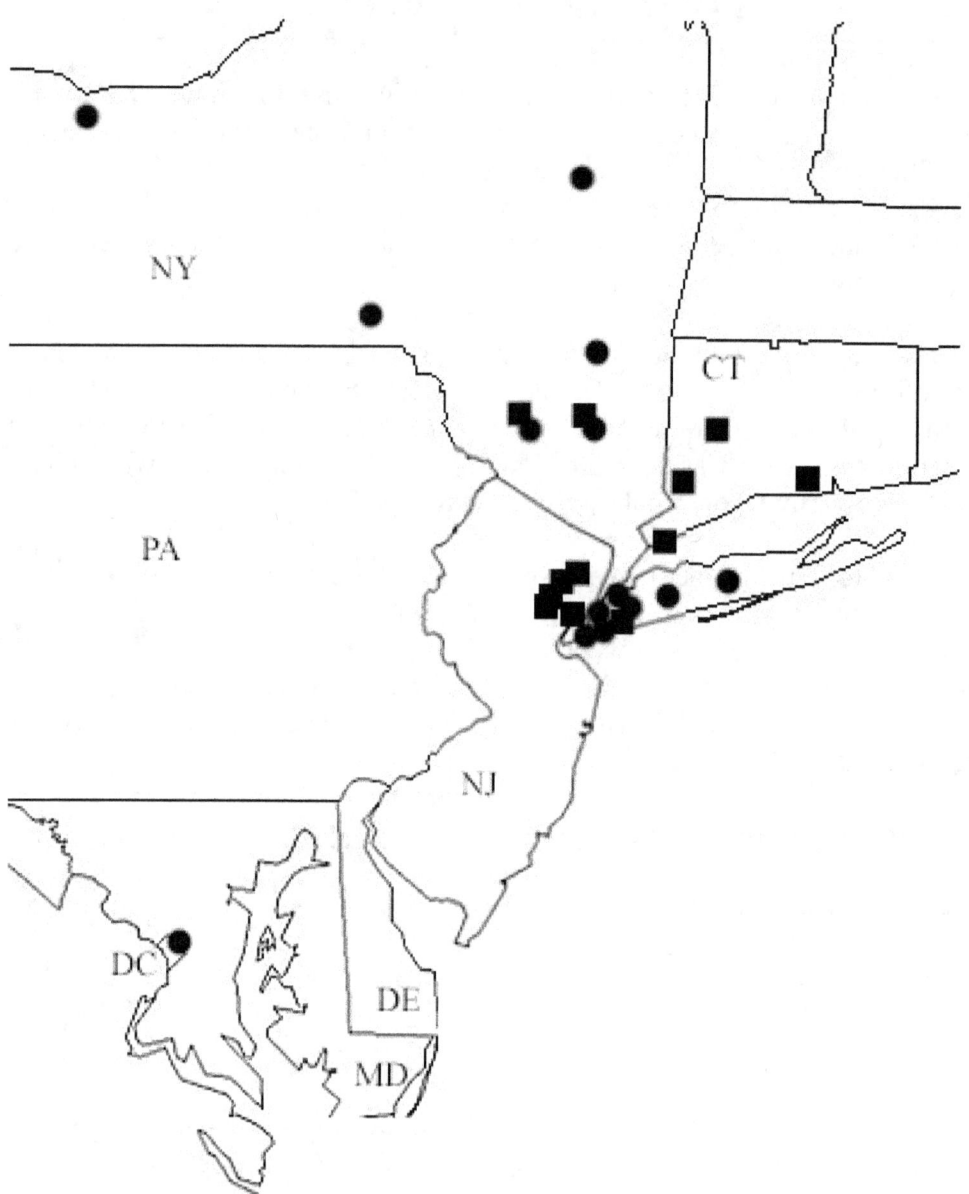

This outline map is a section of a free map found at http://z.about.com/d/geography/1/0/9/H/usa3.jpg

The squares denote places associated with Adolph's family.
The circles denote places associated with John's family.
Honolulu, Hawaii and Belfast, Maine are other places family members lived at this time.

Section I

The Stories and Genealogical Summaries

Chapter 1

Anton VOGELBACH ca1830 - ca1900
Elisabeth SCHNEEBELI ca1830 - ca1900

In the early 1800s one of our Vogelbach ancestors was quietly raising a family of four children - Alexander, Amelia, Emmanuel, and Anton[1] - near Zürich, Switzerland. Some family documents indicate that the town of Küsnacht on the shores of Lake Zürich may have been our ancestral village.[2]

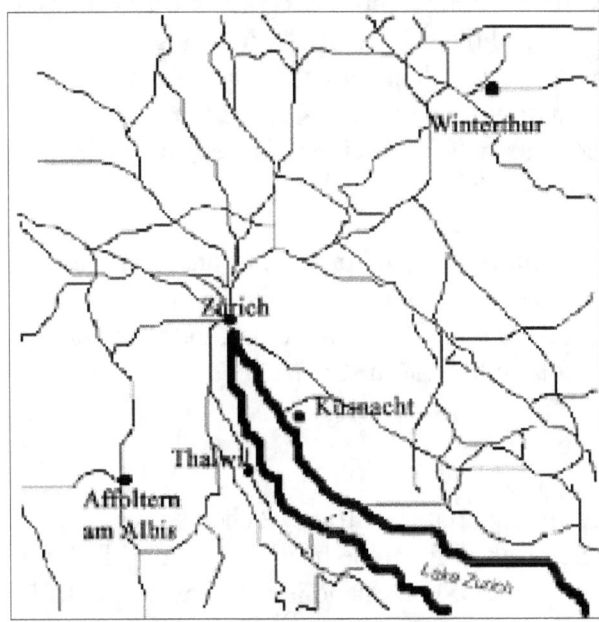

Affoltern am Albis - birthplace of Elisabeth Schneebeli
Küsnacht - birthplace of John Vogelbach.
Thalwil - birthplace of Fanny Moritz
Winterthur - birthplace of other Moritz siblings

We do not know the occupation of this ancestor, but farming or woodworking would be good guesses. Every family at that time had at least a small kitchen garden in which they grew vegetables for their table, even if they did not call themselves farmers. Or, our ancestor could have been some sort of woodworker because we know a few Vogelbach descendants plied the trades of carpenter and stair builder.

Perhaps our ancestor and the other villagers of Küsnacht were going about their daily business when a messenger suddenly arrived in the town square and posted a threatening notice. In essence it might have said, "Join Napoleon's army or suffer imprisonment and death." Napoleon, who was trying to conquer Europe and Russia to

---

[1] These names are from a Family Tree prepared by Charles Oscar Roebuck in 1987 entitled "VOGELBACH - A Swiss who served with Napoleon in the Russian campaign for seven years." Charles did research in Zürich.
[2] Marriage Certificate for John Vogelbach and Fanny Moritz, NYC Health Dept. Record # 65933, 21 Nov 1886, uses the spelling "Kussnach." Küssnacht (with ss), also called Küsnacht at the Rigi, lies many miles away in the canton Schwyz, says Thomas Neukom of the Swiss Archives in an email 30 Jul 2003. Neukom says Küsnacht on Lake Zürich is the more likely birthplace of our ancestor.

make himself emperor of the entire region, needed a continuous supply of men to replace the soldiers being slaughtered by people defending their own villages. If a village was part of a kingdom conquered by Napoleon, or one which had surrendered to his army, then its male residents were subject to conscription, or forced military service, into Napoleon's army as it fought against other kingdoms.

The Napoleonic Wars (1803-1815) began with Napoleon's repeated intervention in Italy, Germany, the Helvetic Republic (Switzerland), and the Netherlands, with the ultimate aim of conquering Great Britain. In 1805, when Napoleon proclaimed himself King of Italy and annexed part of Italy to France, his enemies in Great Britain, Austria, Russia and Sweden formed an alliance called The Third Coalition against him with mixed success.[3]

Meanwhile, Napoleon continued to press men from defeated countries into military service to replenish his forces. Warfare between Napoleon's armies and Russia went on until Russia submitted to him on 14 June 1807. The Russians found the economic repercussions under Napoleon intolerable and rebelled against Napoleon in mid 1812. This time Napoleon's armies were decimated by Russia's scorched earth tactic in which the Russians withdrew and burned their own villages as Napoleon's army pursued them, leaving the invading soldiers with no shelter, food, or supplies on their attack as well as their retreat. Napoleon's starving, cold, and dying soldiers, many of whom had been unwilling members of the army to begin with, slowly wound their way home. Our ancestor somehow survived his trek home across Europe and all the hunger and deprivations of military life.

Imagine the Vogelbach family's joy at seeing their father return home. Our ancestor was one of the lucky ones who made it home alive, though he was probably scarred for life by his experience of the killing, burning, filth, and disease of war. After his return, his wife and children must have tried very hard to help him reclaim his life in Küsnacht.

Those were the formative years of his son, Anton.

Born about 1830, Anton Vogelbach grew up learning his father's trade. When he was a young man, he met a woman named Elizabeth Schneebeli from the nearby town of Affoltern am Albis.[4] Anton and Elizabeth were married in Zürich, Switzerland in the 1850's, and had at least six children: Alexander, Otto, Robert, Adolph, John, and Mary.[5] Anton and Elizabeth were strict Catholic parents.

---

[3] The Columbia Encyclopedia, Sixth Ed, online at http://www.bartleby.com/65/na/Napoleon1.html
[4] Vogelbach Family Tree drawn by Charles Oscar Roebuck in 1987 says Elizabeth was from Affoltern am Albis. Charles researched our European forbears in the records of the Catholic Augustinian Church in Zürich in the 1970's. He learned that all Catholics from the area around Zürich were required by the government in the mid-1800s to register their family at a centrally located Catholic church.
[5] Charles Roebuck's Family Tree also provides us with the names of Anton's children.

The only children of Anton whose lives we know anything about are Adolph and John. Both men immigrated to New York when they were about twenty years old, at least in part to get away from their strict Catholic upbringing. All the stories that have been passed down to us are consistent on this point.

The photo above shows Anton Vogelbach in Switzerland about 1880 with three of his children. The children are not identified, but we believe the girl's name is Mary. The photo is from Peter Heidtmann's collection, and is the only photo of Anton that our family has. Anton Vogelbach's son John either brought the photo with him from Switzerland, or someone sent it to him after he left Europe. It is a poignant and evocative memento of our Swiss ancestors.

Genealogical Summary

A. ANTON[4] **VOGELBACH** was born in the first half of the nineteenth century near Zürich, Switzerland. His ancestors were originally from Germany.[6] About 1850 or so, Anton married ELISABETH SCHNEEBELI,[7] a woman from Affoltern am Albis, and they had at least six children.[8] Anton and Elisabeth's death dates are unknown. They did not immigrate to the USA.

Known children of Anton Vogelbach and Elisabeth Schneebeli are:

+ **1.** i. ADOLPH[1] VOGELBACH (*Anton*[4]) was born in July 1858[9] in Küsnacht, Switzerland and died in 1926 in Crawford, NY.[10] Adolph left Europe about 1880[11] and married BARBARA HASSLER on 23 Dec 1883 in Manhattan, NY.[12] Barbara was born in March 1865[13] in Ulm, Germany and died in 1957 in Crawford Township, NY.[14] Both Adolph and Barbara are buried in the Brick Church Cemetery in Montgomery, NY.[15] They had ten children, but only five survived to adulthood.

---

[6] The name Vogelbach is German, not Swiss, according to several Swiss websites. It is unknown when, why, or from what German region the family may have originally immigrated to Switzerland.

[7] Marriage Certificate for John Vogelbach and Fanny Moritz, *op.cit.*, states that John's mother's name is Elisabeth Schnaebel. Charles Roebuck's Family Tree says "Elizabeth Schnebeli" was born in Affoltern am Albis. Swiss Archives, Zürich www.staatsarchiv.zh.ch/kontakt.php, said Schneebeli is the usual spelling of the name in Affoltern am Albis, Canton Zürich.

[8] Vogelbach Family Tree drawn by Charles Oscar Roebuck in 1987.

[9] Adolph Vogelbach Household, 1900 Census, NY, Orange County, town of Crawford, ED5, sheet 1A

[10] Vogelbach Family Tree drawn by Charles Oscar Roebuck in 1987.

[11] Adolph Vogelbach Household, 1900 Census, *op.cit.*

[12] NYC Marriage Register entry for Adolph Vogelbach and "Babetta Haszler," 1883, Liber 7, No.7634, p 191.

[13] Adolph Vogelbach Household, 1900 Census, NY Orange County, *op.cit.*

[14] Vogelbach Family Tree drawn by Charles Oscar Roebuck in 1987.

[15] Charles Oscar Roebuck, note to author 22 June 2009.

+   **2.**   ii.   JOHN VOGELBACH was born 24 April 1862[16,17] in Küsnacht, Switzerland[18] and died 8 Nov 1947 in Central Islip, NY.[19] John immigrated to the United States about 1882.[20] He married FANNY MORITZ on 21 Nov 1886 in Manhattan.[21] Fanny was born on 5 April 1866 in Thalwil, Switzerland.[22] She died 24 Sept 1927 in Kings Park, NY[23] and is buried with her husband in Friends Cemetery, Westbury, NY.[24] They had thirteen children, though five died in infancy or very early childhood.[25]

3.   iii.   ALEXANDER VOGELBACH was born in Switzerland. Nothing more is known about him.[26]

4.   iv.   OTTO VOGELBACH was born in Switzerland. Nothing more is known about him.

5.   v.   ROBERT VOGELBACH was born in Switzerland. Nothing more is known about him.

6.   vi.   MARY VOGELBACH was born in Switzerland. Nothing more is known about her.

---

[16] John Vogelbach Household, 1900 census, NY, Orange County, Town of Montgomery, ED 28, Sheet 13A.

[17] Central Islip Psychiatric Center Register of Deaths, John Vogelbach, Reg. No. 465, 8 Nov 1947. Documents John's date of birth and his date of death.

[18] Marriage Certificate for John Vogelbach and Fanny Moritz, *op.cit.*

[19] Central Islip Psychiatric Center Register of Deaths, John Vogelbach, *op.cit.*.

[20] John Vogelbach Household, 1900 census, *op.cit.*, sets 1882 as year of immigration for John; he told the census taker he was in the US for 18 years.

[21] Marriage Certificate for John Vogelbach and Fanny Moritz, *op.cit.*

[22] email from Swiss Archives: there is a record of Fanny's family in Ansässenverzeichnis von Thalwil (E III 121.19) and this record states that Amalie Fanny was born on 5 April 1866 in Thalwil.

[23] Kings Park State Hospital Registry of Death for Fanny Vogelbach: Fanny died 24 Sept 1927.

[24] Friends Cemetery Records, Westbury, NY, Section 2, Row 2, Plot 34, Grave 1 and 2.

[25] Birth Certificate for Martha Vogelbach, NYC Health Dept #4698, 28 Mat 1907, says Fanny had 12 previous births, so Martha was Fanny's thirteenth child.

[26] Vogelbach Family Tree drawn by Charles Oscar Roebuck in 1987 gives us names of these four children of Anton and Elizabeth.

Chapter 2

Adolph VOGELBACH 1858 - 1926
Barbara HASSLER 1865 - 1959

1890 photos of Adolph Vogelbach and Barbara Hassler,
from the collection of Charles Roebuck. Used with permission.

Adolph Vogelbach and Barbara Hassler were typical hard-working immigrants who came to New York in the late nineteenth century. Like many Swiss and German immigrants, they sailed from Western Europe and settled in Manhattan among their fellow countrymen. Relatives or fellow countrymen probably helped them find suitable mates; they married and had many children, some of whom died of illness in childhood. This chapter is devoted to Adolph and Barbara and will describe some of the details of their life together.

Adolph, the son of Anton Vogelbach, was born July 1858 in Switzerland.[1] He was a coppersmith, a trade he learned either in Switzerland before he left home or in Manhattan after he arrived in the USA. As a coppersmith, Adolph made useful articles such as handcrafted pots and pans, lanterns, weather vanes, or building materials. Some New York City coppersmiths made cupolas to protect and decorate many rooftops in the city. It is interesting to note that copper was the earliest metal to be worked by human beings,[2] so Adolph's type of work was an ancient and honorable way to make a living.

Immigration and Naturalization

Adolph left Switzerland for New York in 1880.[3] His name has not been definitively located on any ship's passenger list, which is unfortunate for our research, since passenger lists often provide a wealth of family history. Besides the name and type of vessel, passenger lists often reveal the ports of embarkation and debarkation, names of traveling companions, exact date of arrival into the United States, sometimes even the number of pieces of luggage the traveler owned. Perhaps Adolph traveled on a steamship, because steam engines became popular for powering trans-Atlantic vessels in the mid-1800s. Some of these ships did have sails as well, but only to assist the steam engines. The nineteenth century was an important era of transition in sea transportation. Voyages at that time could last anywhere from a week to a month, depending on the weather in the North Atlantic and the type of vessel one traveled on.

A tantalizing clue to Adolph's immigration appears on an 1888 naturalization index card in the National Archives. The card says an Adolf Vogel, Swiss coppersmith living in Manhattan, immigrated to the USA in May 1880 and was naturalized on 11 October 1888.[4] These facts coincide with information we gather about Adolph from the 1900 and 1920 US censuses. Many searches for an Adolf Vogel or Vogelbach, or any number of variant spellings, have so far yielded only one name in the passenger records of 1880, but it is not a definitive match for our ancestor. The passenger record is for a Mr. Adolphe Vogelbach,[5] farmer, originally either from Germany or Switzerland, who arrived in New York on 1 May 1880. His age is obscured. He was not traveling with anyone, apparently. What makes this record less than convincing is that this Adolphe Vogelbach sailed from Macao, Brazil, and

---

[1] Adolph Vogelbach Household, 1900 Census, NY, Orange County, Town of Crawford, ED5 sheet 1A, says Adolph was born in 1858, though his tombstone at the Brick Church Cemetery, Montgomery, NY, says 1859.
[2] http://en.wikipedia.org/wiki/Coppersmith and http://www.rameria.com/inglese/history.html
[3] Adolph Vogelbach Household, 1900 Census, *op.cit*, says Adolph immigrated in 1880.
  Adolph Vogelbach Household, 1910 Census, NJ, Hudson County, 4-WD Kearny, ED 243, Sheet 6A, says Adolph immigrated in 1879.
  Adolph Vogelbach Household, 1920 Census, CT, Essex, Middlesex County, ED 212 Sheet 12A, says Adolph immigrated in 1880 and was naturalized in 1888.
[4] Common Pleas Court, New York County, Vol 657, Record 76, Adolf Vogel, 11 Oct 1888.
[5] Levinia F. Warren Passenger List on Ancestry.com, lists Mr. Adolphe Vogelbach, farmer, either German or Swiss, who arrived in New York from Macao, Brazil on 1 May 1880.

there are no family stories hinting that our Adolph first stopped in Brazil before arriving in New York City.

Adolph's wife Barbara Hassler was born in Ulm,[6] Germany on 26 March 1865, and census records say that she immigrated in 1882.[7] That would make her about 17 when she left Europe. Charles Roebuck said, "Barbara's brother Jacob preceded her to the U.S. and worked to pay for her passage. Her mother and father and younger sister Mary came over later, after Barbara and Jacob paved the way." Family lore says that that Barbara met Adolph "on the boat" to America in 1881.[8] Information mentioned on census reports contradicts this, but censuses sometimes give incorrect immigration information. (Actually, the only reliable information on a census report is where a family was living when the census taker knocked on the door.) In any case, Adolph and Barbara married in Manhattan in December 1883 when he was 24 and she was 20.[9] Adolph was employed as a coppersmith when they were married, and the marriage registry says they were living at 1420 Ave A.[10]

Adolph and Barbara had ten children, but only five of them survived past infancy or early childhood. It seems that five infants died between 1884 and 1900.[11,12] Such a high infant mortality in one family is quite rare today, but Barbara probably knew many women who suffered similar tragedies. Many infant deaths in New York City were due to the rapid spread of diseases in the poor and densely populated areas of the city. When infants got sick, hospitals rarely admitted them; families were usually left to their own treatment methods. Even antibiotics available to family doctors were largely ineffective. Penicillin, for example, was discovered in 1928, long after Barbara may have needed it to treat her children.

---

[6] In an email on 4 Feb 2003, Charles Roebuck said Barbara Hassler was born in Ulm, Germany.

[7] Adolph Vogelbach Household, 1900 Census, *op.cit.* Barbara was born in Germany in March 1865 and immigrated in 1882.

[8] Barbara's name has not yet been found on a ship's passenger list in the period 1880 to 1882. If we could find one of their names, we could search the rest of the passenger list for a name resembling the other person's, to prove or disprove the old family story.

[9] NYC Marriage Register for Adolph Vogelbach and Babetta Haszler, 1883, Liber 7, No.7634, p191, recorded Jan 2, 1884, says date of marriage was 23 Dec 1883.

[10] NYC Marriage Register for Adolph Vogelbach and Babetta Haszler, *op.cit*, documents their address and Adolph's occupation. It also says Adolph's father was Anton, mother Elizabeth Schneberi. (Close enough!) Babetta Haszler's parents were Johan G. and Annette Steller. (Charles Roebuck said Barbara's mother's name was really Anne-Marie Stedder, according to a family bible and a cemetery headstone. The family also prefers the spelling Hassler to Haszler.) Officiating minister was Adolph Berckmann. The minister's name could be researched in NYC Directories to determine his religion and name of his church.

[11] Adolph Vogelbach Household, 1900 US Census, *op.cit,* says that Barbara had given birth to 9 children, but only four of them were alive at the time of the census. Fanny would be born in 1903, and she is the fifth surviving child.

[12] Charles Oscar Roebuck's Family Tree, created in 1987, lists the names of the children who died before 1900: Adolph, Martha, two boys named Maximillian, and Olga. Some of them died during a diphtheria epidemic, he said.

Adolph's Family Residences 1883-1958

1883	Adolph and Barbara	1420 Ave A, NYC	The couple's first residence together.
Jan 1888	Adolph, Barbara, and son Robert	East New York, Brooklyn	This is where Robert was born on 23 Jan 1888.[13]
Oct 1888	Adolph, Barbara, and Robert	Morris Ave, Manhattan	What are believed to be Adolph's citizenship papers say he lived at Morris Ave., NYC on 11 Oct 1888.[14]
ca.1896 - 1900	Adolph, Barbara, Robert, Elfrieda, Oscar, and Edmund	Crawford, near Montgomery in Orange County, NY[15]	Oscar was born in Crawford on 25 Jan 1897.[16] Edmund was born in Crawford on 21 March 1899.[17]
ca.1909	Robert	Queens	Robert married Friederika Waechter in 1909 and lived in Queens.[18]
1910 – ca. 1916	Adolph, Barbara, Elfrieda, Oscar, Edmund, and Fannie	546 Devon St., Kearny, NJ	They had a mortgage on a home at this address[19] and they seem to have kept up ownership even as they continued to move. Elfrieda remained in NJ, fell in love, and married there.[20]
ca.1911	Elfrieda	Kearny, NJ	Elfrieda married Fred Anderson
ca.1916 - 1917	Adolph, Barbara, Edmund, and Fannie	West New York, NJ and Jamaica, Queens	Family lore has Adolph and Barbara residing in these two places before WWI.
1917	Robert	49 Overlook, Newburgh	Robert had moved upstate by now.[21]
1918	Oscar	131 Gidney Ave, Newburgh, NY	Oscar & Eleanor Lindsay lived in Newburgh NY as newlyweds[22]

---

[13] Robert Vogelbach's WW I Draft Registration Card A, on Ancestry.com, says he was born in East New York, NY, 23 Jan 1888, so a conclusion would be that Adolph's family lived in Brooklyn in Jan 1888.

[14] Adolph Vogelbach Household, 1920 Census, *op.cit*, says 1888 was yr of Adolph's naturalization. If the Adolf mentioned in footnote #4 is our relative, then Adolph's naturalization was 11 Oct 1888 at the Court of Common Pleas in Manhattan. That naturalization document says Adolf lived at Morris Ave. Manhattan.

[15] Adolph Vogelbach Household, 1900 Census, *op.cit*, lists Adolph, farmer, wife Barbara, and their children Robert 11 , Elfrieda 9, Oscar 3, and Edmund 1   (Charles Roebuck lives near this farm today.)

[16] Birth Certificate for Oscar Vogelbach, NYS Dept of Health Certif# D131535, Oscar was born 25 Jan 1897 in the Town of Montgomery, Orange County, NY.

[17] WW I Draft Registration Card for Edmund Vogelbach, on Ancestry.com, Ser No 783, Order No A-2986, dated 12 Sep 1918, says Edmund was born 21 Mar 1899.

[18] Robert Vogelbach Household, 1910 census, NY Queens ED-1255 Sheet 13B, by 28 Apr 1910, Robert & Frieda had been married for one year.

[19] Adolph Vogelbach Household, 1910 census, NJ, Hudson County, Kearny Ward 4, ED 243, Sheet 6A, residence was 546 Devon St.

[20] Marriage Record for Oscar Vogelbach & Eleanor Lindsay, Town of Kearny, Hudson Co, NJ, married on 6 Mar 1918. Certified copy of the marriage record is in the collection of Charles Roebuck. WWI Draft Card for Edmund Vogelbach, *op.cit*., says Edmund was living at 171 Laurel Ave, Kearny in 1918.

[21] WWI Draft Card, on Ancestry.com, for Robert Vogelbach dated 5 Jun 1917.

[22] WWI Draft Card, on Ancestry.com, for Oscar Vogelbach dated 5 July 1918.

1918	Edmund	171 Laurel Ave, Kearny, NJ	Edmund, still single, lived in NJ and worked in NYC[23]
1920	Edmund & Elfrieda	24 Park Ave, Lyndhurst, NJ	Edmund lived with his sister Elfrieda's family.[24]
1919	Oscar & Eleanor	207 Devon Street, Kearny, NJ	Oscar moved back to NJ after WWI, and moved into an apt owned by Eleanor's parents.[25]
1918 – ca.1925	Adolph, Barbara, Fanny	New City Street, Essex, CT[26]	Adolph is working as a coppersmith in the Witch Hazel Company in Essex.
1926	Barbara	Crawford, NY	Adolph died in Crawford in 1926.
1927 - 1931	Barbara & Roman	601 Bergen St, Newark, NJ[27]	Barbara married Roman Thoenig and they lived in Newark. He died in 1931.
1930	Oscar & Eleanor	23 William St, North Arlington, NJ[28]	Oscar, Eleanor, and children Ethel & Robert.
1932 - ?	Barbara	Newark, NJ	Barbara lived in an apartment in Newark for a while.[29]
1942	Robert & Frieda	170 Preston St, Ridgefield Park, NJ	Robert lived in NJ but worked in NYC.[30] He eventually bought a farmhouse in Crawford which had been built in the mid 1800s. In 1957 they moved to St. Petersburg, FL. Robert died there in 1969.
ca.1942	Basically, North Arlington was the family residence in 1942.	38 Park Ave., North Arlington, NJ	Barbara moved in with Oscar in Kearny; he worked in Bayonne; for a little while Eleanor lived in Montgomery NY.[31]
1953	Barbara Hassler Vogelbach Thoenig	546 Devon St, Arlington, NJ	Barbara Thoenig said she lived in Kearny.[32]
1946 - 1959	Barbara Thoenig	Crawford, NY	Barbara returned with Oscar to Crawford. This is where she died and was buried.

Adolph, Barbara, and their children lived in Orange County, NY in the late 1890s and early 1900s, probably to be near Barbara's parents who owned a farm in Searsville, Town of Crawford, in Orange County. Perhaps everyone thought it would help Barbara recover from the deaths of five children. Adolph was not a successful farmer, however, and the family lived in various places after that, eventually settling in Kearny, New Jersey."[33]

---

[23] Edmund Vogelbach's WWI Draft Card, 1917, on Ancestry.com.

[24] Fred Anderson Household, 1920 Census, NJ, Bergen County, Lyndhurst, ED 185, Sheet 16A.

[25] Oscar Vogelbach Household, 1920 Census, NJ, Hudson County, Kearny, ED 274, Sheet 21 A, and a note to author in June 2009 from Charles Roebuck.

[26] Adolph Vogelbach Household, 1920 Census, CT, Essex, Middlesex County, ED 212, Sheet 12 A.

[27] Roman Thoenig Household, 1930 Census, NJ, Essex County, Newark, 6th Ward, ED 7-280, Sheet 12B.

[28] Oscar Vogelbach Household, 1930 Census, NJ, Bergen County, N Arlington, ED 2-173, Sheet 9B.

[29] Contributed by Barbara Vogelbach

[30] Robert Vogelbach's WWII Draft Card 1942 on Ancestry.com.

[31] Oscar Vogelbach's WWII Draft card 1942 on Ancestry.com provides all these details.

[32] Record of Birth for Oscar Vogelbach, Certificate# D131535, NYS Dept of Health, Albany, dated 24 Jul 1953, States that Oscar was born 25 Jan 1897 in Orange County, Village of Montgomery. Sworn on 25 May 1953 by Barbara Thoenig, mother, residing at 546 Devon St, Arlington NJ, Bergen County.

[33] E-mail from Charles Roebuck on 6 January 2007.

The photo above was taken by the author in 2009. This was Adolph and Barbara's farmhouse for a few years around the turn of the 19th to 20th century. Besides dairy farming, they also took in boarders. Their son Oscar was born here, and possibly a couple of other children as well. Oscar attended a one-room school house and made lifelong friends there. The farmhouse is located on Route 17K in the Town of Crawford in Orange County, New York (about equidistant from the hamlets of Montgomery and Bullville). It was only two or three miles from the farm owned and run by Barbara's parents and her older brother Jacob. Adolph Vogelbach failed as a farmer, and the family moved back to the city which allowed Adolph to return to work as a coppersmith.[34] Years later their son Oscar returned to the area and established his own family on a farm next door to his Hassler grandparents. A number of Adolph's descendants still live in the Town of Crawford.

Adolph had between 25-50 head of Holstein dairy cows on about one or two hundred acres of land, enough for a family to make a good living. In the early 1900s farmers took their milk to one of a number of different local creameries, where it was bottled and then distributed locally. From the 1950s onward, the creameries came to farms with large trucks to pick up the milk (the kind of trucks you see on the road that have large metal container-like bodies (such as the type that carry heating oil). During that time most farmers had a large tank in their milkhouses where the milk was stored until pick-up. These tanks were refrigerated and had a device like a large mixer that kept the milk circulating so that the cream would not separate out.

---

[34] Adolph Vogelbach Household, 1910 Census, *op.cit*, Adolph owned his own coppersmith business.
   Adolph Vogelbach Household, 1920 Census, CT, Essex, Middlesex County, ED 212 Sheet 12A, says Adolph worked as a coppersmith at the Witch Hazel Co. in Middlesex, CT.

Charles Roebuck says, "This was the type of set-up that my father had when he farmed until 1973. The milk was not pasteurized on site--pasteurization was done at the creameries. When I was growing up on the farm, we never even drank pasteurized milk. My father had a very clean dairy and trusted the quality of his milk, so there was no need to pasteurize it. Nothing tastes as good as whole, raw milk! But--if farmers are the least bit dirty, their milk could be contaminated."

Robert Is Born

Robert was born in 1888. He was not their firstborn, though; Barbara's first son, named Adolph after his father, died when he was very young. Robert survived and grew up as the oldest child, and was also the first to get married. He met a woman named Friederika Waechter. She was a year younger than he, and her parents were Swiss and German, just like Robert's parents. They probably had a lot in common with regard to family traditions and habits. They married in Queens in 1909. Robert was working as an accountant at the time in Queens. He and Frieda lived at 47 Oceanview Ave., Queens, NY,[35] which was only about a half-hour walk from his Uncle John Vogelbach's family.

They adopted[36] a girl named Helen. She was their only child.

After a few years, Robert moved his young family to Orange County, NY, and they lived at 49 Overlook, Newburgh. Robert worked as an accountant for the Kells Company in Newburgh. World War I broke out, and Robert registered for the draft in 1917; thankfully, he did not have to leave Frieda and Helen and go into the armed forces.[37]

After World War I, Robert moved his family to Queens again, to 64 Yale Avenue, Jamaica, and Robert took a job as an accountant in a coffee house.[38] Around 1925, the family moved to Ridgefield Park, NJ, and Robert began to commute into Manhattan for work. First, he was the secretary of Medropa Travel Tourist Bureau, Inc. in Manhattan,[39] and then, for the rest of his career, he worked for Kalek Water Company of NY, Inc.[40]

When Grace Vogelbach was job hunting after graduating high school in 1937, she made an unannounced visit to Robert at the Kalek Water Co. Robert was her father's first cousin. He

---

[35] Robert Vogelbach Household, 1910 Census, NY, Queens, ED 1255, Sheet 13B.
[36] Source: Charles Roebuck.
[37] WW I Draft Registration Card for Robert Vogelbach dated 5 Jun 1917, Ancestry.com.
  Robert Vogelbach Household, 1930 Census, NJ, Bergen County, Ridgefield Park, ED 2-182, Sheet 12B, says Robert was not a veteran of WWI.
[38] Robert Vogelbach Household, 1920 Census, , NY, Queens, AD 4, ED 300, Sheet 17B.
[39] Manhattan Directory 1925, on Ancestry.com, Robert Vogelbach, occupation: Secretary of Medropa Travel Tourist Bureau, Inc., home in Ridgefield Park, NJ.
[40] WW II Draft Registration Card 1942, on Ancestry.com, Ser.#1253, employment Kalek Water Co of NY, Inc., business address was 30 Rockefeller Plaza, NYC.

graciously took Grace out to lunch, though he had not expected the visit. Grace thought he may have owned the company.[41] (He did not. Unfortunately, he did not have a job for her, either.)

Charles Roebuck said:[42]

> "The name of the company that my Granduncle Robert Vogelbach worked for was the Kalak Water Company. It was located at 6 Church Street in lower Manhattan at one point. I don't know if that address still exists, because it would be very close to where the Trade Center was. It's even possible that when the Trade Center was first built, that area was demolished to become part of the complex. My mother happened to have an old envelope among her things that had the name and address of the company. She knew right off the name of the company, but wasn't sure how it was spelled, but then she remembered she might still have the envelope.

> "Robert Vogelbach also eventually bought a home up in the Montgomery/Searsville area, about a 1/2 mile from where my grandfather, his younger brother Oscar, lived. My Aunt Barbara (my mother's younger sister) now lives in this farmhouse. She and her husband Walter Roebuck bought it in 1956. Robert and Frieda stayed on there for a year, in an apartment in the home, and then moved to Florida."

Robert Vogelbach died in Jan 1969 in St. Petersburg, FL.[43] Friederika died on 4 Feb 1977 in a nursing home in Andover, NJ.[44] In her last years, she had been living near her daughter Helen, her grandchildren, and other family members.

Adolph and Barbara's Oldest Daughter, Elfrieda

Elfrieda was born in Feb 1891,[45] probably while the family was still living in Manhattan. She worked for a couple of years after high school in a dressmaker company. Frieda met and married Fred Anderson about 1911, probably in Kearny, NJ, where the Vogelbach family was living at the time. Fred was a native of New Jersey; he was born there about 1888. The Anderson family lived for a time in Lyndhurst, NJ, at 34 Park Ave. which was about four miles from where Frieda used to live in Kearny. Fred worked in Lyndhurst as a furniture salesman. Frieda's younger brother Edmund Vogelbach lived with her family after World War I and before he got married. Edmund was a bookkeeper at the same furniture company where his brother-in-law Fred Anderson was the salesman. Frieda and Fred Anderson had

---

[41] Conversation with Grace Vogelbach, April 2002
[42] Email from Charles Roebuck to the author 19 May 2002.
[43] Social Security Death Index, Ancestry.com, Robert's birth and death information.
[44] Social Security Death Index, Ancestry.com, Friederika's birth and death information.
[45] Adolph Vogelbach Household, 1900 Census, *op.cit.*

three children, Frederick, born 1912, Edmund, born 1913, and Elfrieda Marguerette, born 1915.[46]

Elfrieda Vogelbach Anderson died very young either in NJ or CT; she was only in her late thirties, and Fred remarried a woman named Mary Cannon. His children, his new wife, and her two children, along with two servants, lived in Greenwich, CT. He was apparently doing well financially, because he owned a nice home there on River Side Ave, and owned a dry goods store in town.[47]

Oscar Vogelbach

Oscar Vogelbach was born soon after the family moved up to Montgomery, Orange County, NY. He was born on 25 Jan 1897 and baptized in September of that year in the Reformed Church of Montgomery.[48, 49]

After high school, when he was about nineteen, Oscar lived on the Upper West Side of Manhattan. He was already working as an engineer.[50] At the time, his parents were living in

Kearny, NJ. One winter day while visiting his family, he was ice skating and met Eleanor Woods Lindsay whose family also lived in Kearny.[51] The couple married in Kearny, NJ in the Knox Presbyterian Church in 1918.[52]

The couple was striking. Oscar was tall and slender with brown eyes and brown hair,[53] and Eleanor was very beautiful. This photo is of Oscar and Eleanor circa 1918, from the collection of Charles Roebuck, and is used with his permission.

---

[46] Fred Anderson Household, 1920 Census, NJ, Bergen County, Lyndhurst, ED 185, Sheet 16A

[47] Fred Anderson Household. 1930 Census, CT, Fairfield County, Greenwich Town, ED 139, Sheet 4B.

[48] Certificate of Baptism for Oscar Vogelbach, Reformed Church of Montgomery, NY, copy in the collection of Charles Roebuck, dated 9 July 1953: Oscar Vogelbach, a "son of Edel Vogelbach and his wife Barbara Haslett," was born on 25 Jan 1897, baptized 2 Sept 1897 by Rev. J Frederic Berg.

[49] Oscar Vogelbach Birth Record, NYS Dept of Health Certificate # D131535.

[50] Manhattan Directory 1916, Ancestry.com, Oscar is an engineer living at 520 W145th Street, Manhattan.

[51] E-mail from Charles Roebuck dated 6 Jan 2007.

[52] Marriage Certificate for Oscar Vogelbach & Eleanor Lindsay, Dept of Health, Town of Kearny, Hudson Countu, NJ, Oscar Vogelbach, 21, married Eleanor Woods Lindsay, 19, on 6 Mar 1918 before Rev. Robert T. Graham in the Knox Presbyterian Church.

[53] WW I Draft Registration Card for Oscar Vogelbach, dated 5 Jun 1918, on Ancestry.com.

Soon after their marriage, the newlyweds moved to Newburgh, NY where Oscar found a job in the Newburgh Shipyard.[54] They moved back to New Jersey about 1919, directly after World War I ended, and lived in an apartment owned by Eleanor's parents. In 1920, Oscar worked as an engineer on a project for the local school district in North Arlington.[55] They saved enough money to buy a farmhouse and some acreage in Montgomery, NY.

Charles Oscar Roebuck told this story[56] about his grandfather:

> "My grandfather Oscar and grandmother Eleanor had bought the 'farm' in Montgomery in the early 1920s so that his parents, Adolph and Barbara, could live there. Oscar's family visited on weekends and used it as a summer place until 1937, when they moved up here (Montgomery, NY) full time. Oscar bought additional acres during the 1940s, creating a real working farm. The place was farmed first by his son Robert from after World War II to 1952. Around 1950, my father, Charles Roebuck, started helping Robert, and then took over the farm completely in 1952, at which time Robert began working as an engineer.

> "My grandfather, however, continued to commute daily (he was a pioneer in commuting, it seems) to New Jersey to his office--about 1-1/2 to 2 hours one way. He continued to do that until just before World War II,[57] when he became one of the chief engineers working to ready the Bayonne Naval Base and Brooklyn Navy Yard for the war effort. He was so busy with that work that he couldn't commute daily--so my grandmother Eleanor moved back down to North Arlington, New Jersey with their two youngest children (Barbara and Ted).

> "My mother, Ethel Vogelbach, was already living down in New Jersey. She worked for a while for her father. But then, because of government regulations prohibiting relatives from working together, she got a very good job working for contractors building Camp Kilmer (around New Brunswick, NJ), which became one of the major embarkation points for soldiers heading to Europe. So, during the war years, from about 1942-1945 or 1946, the whole family was living back in New Jersey--although my grandmother brought the two younger kids up to the farm almost every weekend because they hated living down in the "city." When my grandmother and the kids

---

[54] WW I Draft Registration Card for Oscar Vogelbach Ancestry.com, Oscar was employed at Newburgh Shipyard, New Windsor NY. He and Eleanor lived at 131 Gidney Ave, Newburgh NY

[55] Oscar Vogelbach Household, 1930 census, NJ Bergen County, North Arlington, ED-173 Sheet 9B, Oscar was an engineer doing a project for a school district, either in N. Arlington or in Newark. They had a boarder, Noble Armstrong, whose work was "construction, school district," perhaps on Oscar's project.

[56] E-mail from Charles Roebuck on 6 Jan 2007 and a note in June 2009.

[57] WWII Draft Registration card for Oscar Vogelbach 1942, Ancestry.com, Ser No. U 671, Oscar said his telephone number was Kearny 2-4396W. He was employed by Wigton-Abbott Corp, Mahony-Troast Construction Co, and August Arace & Sons, doing contract work at the Bayonne Naval Supply Depot. His contact person was his wife, Mrs. Eleanor Woods Vogelbach, RFD#3, Montgomery NY.

moved back up here (Montgomery) permanently after the war, my grandfather continued to commute--and he did that until his death in 1959."

After World War II, Oscar became a founding partner of a private engineering consulting company called Vogelbach & Bauman of Plainfield, NJ.[58] Oscar died 27 Dec 1959 in Montgomery, NY.[59] Eleanor died 2 Dec 1983 in Thompson Ridge, NY.[60]

Edmund Vogelbach

Edmund was born in 1899 while the family lived in Crawford.[61] As a young man, he was short and of slender build; he had brown hair and black eyes.[62]

In 1918, Edmund lived in Kearny, NJ, but he commuted to work in Manhattan as a clerk for F. Schumacher & Co., a fine furniture store.[63] His next-of-kin on his WWI draft card was his mother, Barbara Vogelbach who was living pretty far away in the town of Middlesex, CT. He was still single and lucky that he was not drafted into World War I.

About 1920 Edmund moved three miles north to Lyndhurst to live with his sister Elfrieda, her husband Fred Anderson, and their three children.

Edmund married Phyllis Beck in New Jersey about 1924. They moved to Crestwood, NY, in lower Westchester County where they soon had a child, Elizabeth. Edmund continued to work for F. Schumacher & Co. as a clerk and bookkeeper and commuted to and from the Manhattan Schumacher store for a few years.[64]

By the way, F. Schumacher & Co. still exists. There is one store located at Madison Ave. and East 28th Street and another at Third Ave. and East 58th Street. Their website says, "Since 1889, F. Schumacher & Co. has brought its commitment to superb quality and superior design to interiors where only the finest products will suffice, including the White House, the Chambers of the United States Supreme Court and countless distinguished residences."[65] Edmund apparently worked in a very elegant store.

---

[58] E-mail from Gretchen Vogelbach, 25 Oct 2000, "My grandfather was Oscar Vogelbach of Vogelbach & Bauman in Plainfield, NJ. He was from Montgomery, NY, where he owned a dairy farm."
[59] Oscar died 27 Dec 1959, according to his death certificate in the collection of Charles Roebuck.
[60] Social Security Death Index, Ancestry.com, and her death certificate, in the collection of Charles Roebuck.
[61] WW I Draft Registration Card for Edmund Adolph Vogelbach, Ancestry.com, 12 Sep 1918, Ser No 783, born 21 Mar 1899.
[62] WW I Draft Registration Card for Edmund Adolph Vogelbach, *op.cit.*
[63] WW I Draft Registration Card for Edmund Adolph Vogelbach, *op.cit,* Edmund worked as a sample clerk for F. Schumacher & Co at 7 W 37th Street, NYC, but home address was 171 Laurel Ave, Kearny, NJ.
[64] Manhattan Directory 1925,Ancestry.com, Edmund Vogelbach,clerk F. Schumacher & Co.,(h)Crestwood, NY.
[65] http://fschumacher.com/company/default.aspx

Edmund bought a home in Ridgefield, CT, for his young family, but did not live there very long. He died at age 29 or 30.[66] Phyllis married a man named Noble Armstrong who adopted Phyllis and Edmund's daughter Betty. After this time, Phyllis and Betty lost touch with the rest of the Vogelbachs[67] perhaps because they moved to California. In any case, Phyllis died in Oct 1969 in Los Angeles, CA.[68]

The Youngest Child, Fanny

Fanny was born 15 Sept 1903[69] on Long Island, NY.[70] As the youngest, she moved with her parents from Crawford to Jamaica, Queens; to Kearny and West New York, NJ; and finally to Connecticut.

She married Myron Lewis in Connecticut about 1924 and they lived in Southbury, CT, New Haven County, where their seven children were born and raised. She lived in Southbury from the time she married Myron until her death. Myron was born in Southbury, CT in 1900.[71] The Lewis Family goes back several more generations in Southbury. Myron was an insurance agent in 1930.[72] However, he changed jobs and retired as a milling machine operator for Waterbury Farrell Foundry.[73]

Fanny died in 1984 in Southbury, CT.[74] Myron died in Waterbury, CT, in 1992.[75]

Their Children Grown and Married -
Adolph and Barbara Returned to Crawford

Adolph and Barbara moved back to Crawford NY in the early 1920s, before Adolph died in 1926.[76] Ruth Ritter remembers driving upstate when she was about five years old to visit her Grandaunt Barbara; this was probably right after Adolph died. Ruth's father drove the car, and she sat in the back seat with Grandpa John. Ruth remembers going swimming in a lake

---

[66] Phyllis Vogelbach Household, 1930 Census, CT, Fairfield County, Ridgefield Town, ED 173, Sheet 10B, dated 14 May. Phyllis is a widow living with her 4-year old daughter Elizabeth in a home she owned worth $20,000 at 194 Branchville Road.

[67] Source: Charles Roebuck.

[68] Social Security Death Index, Ancestry.com.

[69] Social Security Death Index, Ancestry.com

[70] Adolph Vogelbach Household, 1910 Census, NJ, Hudson County, Kearny, ED 243, Sheet 6A.

[71] Elmer Lewis Household, 1910 Census, CT, New Haven County, Town of Southbury, ED 455, Sheet 4B.

[72] Myron Lewis Household, 1930 Census, CT, New Haven County, Town of Southbury, ED 5-196, Sheet 10A says Myron was 24 and Fanny was 21 when they married.

[73] Connecticut Death Index at Ancestry.com. Myron Lewis death certificate #27553.

[74] Social Security Death Index at Ancestry.com, Fanny Lewis, born 15 Sep 1903, died May 1984 in Southbury.

[75] Social Security Death Index at Ancestry.com, 045-01-4963. Myron b 9 Jul 1900 d 10 Dec 1990 Waterbury.

[76] According to Charles Roebuck, Adolph died in 1926. Charles said, "My Aunt Barbara said he died in Crawford, NY."

in Crawford. They left Grandpa John up there with his sister-in-law Barbara. Ruth has a vivid memory of a crystal set (radio) at Aunt Barbara's house. Olga Jargstorff said her mother Olga Vogelbach told her that Aunt Barbara was somebody they all liked very much! Barbara married a man named Roman Thoenig sometime after Adolph died, and they lived in Newark.[77] It was a brief marriage; Roman died in 1931.

Charles Roebuck says:

> "About 1942 Barbara Hassler moved in with my grandparents into their house at 38 Park Avenue in North Arlington, NJ. For all intents and purposes that was her home-- but she stayed for brief periods of time with her sister Mary.

> "In 1946 she moved up here to the farm in Searsville with her son (Oscar), daughter-in-law (Eleanor) and the family (my Aunt Barbara and Uncle Ted were the only kids then because both my mother and her brother Robert were grown up--although they both stayed at the farm for periods of time.)

> "From 1946 until her death, Barbara Hassler's home was here on the farm---however, as in the period during WW II and just after, from time to time she would go stay with her sister Mary--but her home was up here. Throughout my early childhood until her death she was a strong presence in my life because my grandparents' house on the farm was right next door to a small house that my grandfather had built for my mother and father after they married (the house that I grew up in). It was sort of like a family compound--there was the main farmhouse (originally built in the 1700s). Right next door to it (and connected by out-buildings) was our house. Over the garage (which was between the house and the barn), my grandmother's sister (Ethel Lindsay Lyons Armitage) had an apartment, and their other sister, Margaret, lived there with Ethel after Ethel's husband died. Then there was another small summer house on the property that my grandfather had converted and various family members lived there over the years."[78]

Barbara died in 1959[79] at the advanced age of 94. She outlived two husbands and all but three of her ten children.[80] Barbara, her siblings Jacob and Mary, their parents, her husband Adolph Vogelbach, their son Oscar and his wife Eleanor, Oscar and Eleanor's daughter Ethel Vogelbach Roebuck, and Ethel's husband Charles Roebuck are all buried in The Brick Church Cemetery in Montgomery, NY.[81]

---

[77] Roman Thoenig Household, 1930 Census, NJ, Essex County, Newark, 6th Ward, ED 7-280, Sheet 12B.
[78] email from Charles Roebuck, 3 May 2009.
[79] Barbara's tombstone in The Brick Church Cemetery, Montgomery NY, says 1959.
[80] Surviving her were Robert d. 1969, Oscar d. 1959, and Fanny d. 1984
[81] Note from Charles Roebuck, June 2009.

Genealogical Summary

1. **ADOLPH**[1] **VOGELBACH** (*Anton*[4]) was born in July 1858 in Switzerland[82] and died in 1926 in Crawford, NY.[83] Adolph emigrated from Europe to the United States about 1880[84] and married BARBARA HASSLER on 23 Dec 1883 in Manhattan, NY.[85] Barbara was born in March 1865 in Ulm, Germany[86] and died in 1959.[87] They had ten children.

Known children of Adolph Vogelbach and Barbara Hassler are:

7. i.   ADOLPH[2] VOGELBACH (*Adolph*[1], *Anton*[4]) was born about 1884 in New York and died before 1900.[88]

8. ii.   MARTHA[2] VOGELBACH was born between 1885 and 1896 in New York and died before 1900.

9. iii.   MAXIMILLIAN[2] VOGELBACH I was born between 1885 and 1896 in New York and died before 1900.

10. iv   MAXIMILLIAN[2] VOGELBACH II was born between 1886 and 1896 in New York and died before 1900.

11. v.   OLGA[2] VOGELBACH was born between 1885 and 1896 in New York and died before 1900.

12. vi.   ROBERT[2] VOGELBACH was born 23 Jan 1888[89] in Brooklyn, NY[90] and died in St. Petersburg, FL in January 1969.[91] He married FRIEDERIKA WAECHTER about 1909.[92] Friederika "Frieda" was born 8 June 1887[93] in New York of a Swiss father and German mother.[94] Frieda died in Andover, NJ, on 4 Feb 1977.[95]

---

[82] Adolph Vogelbach Household, 1900 Census, NY, Orange County, town of Crawford, ED5, sheet 1A, says he was born 1858. His tombstone says he was born in 1859, which is probably incorrect.

[83] Vogelbach Family Tree drawn by Charles Roebuck, 1987.

[84] Adolph Vogelbach Household, 1900 Census, *op.cit.*

[85] NYC Marriage Register entry for Adolph Vogelbach and "Babetta Haszler," 1883, Liber 7, No.7634, p 191.

[86] Adolph Vogelbach Household, 1900 Census, *op.cit.*

[87] Tombstone for Barbara Hassler in The Brick Church Cemetery says she died in 1959.

[88] Vogelbach Family Tree by Charles Roebuck gives us names of the five children who died in infancy.

[89] Adolph Vogelbach Household, 1900 Census, *op.cit.*, Robert was born Jan 1889. Social Security Death Index at Ancestry.com says Robert was born 23 Jan 1888.

[90] Robert's WW I Draft Registration Card says he was born in East New York, Brooklyn, 23 Jan 1888.

[91] Social Security Death Index on Ancestry.com

[92] Robert Vogelbach Household, 1910 census NY Queens ED-1255 Sheet 13B, they were married about a year.

[93] Social Security Death Index on Ancestry.com says her birthday was 8 June 1887.

[94] Robert Vogelbach Household, 1910 census, *op.cit.*

[95] Social Security Death Index on Ancestry.com and Charles Roebuck's Family Tree.

The only child of Robert Vogelbach and Friederika Waechter is:

25. i. HELEN[3] VOGELBACH was born 17 Nov 1913 and died Oct 1983 in Maywood, Bergen County, NJ.[96] She was the adopted child of Robert and Frieda. Helen married WILLIAM ECKEL about 1938. William was born in 19 June 1906, and he died in March 1986 in Towaco, Morris County, New Jersey.[97] Helen and William had two children.

13. vii. ELFRIEDA[2] VOGELBACH was born in New York in Feb 1891[98] and died before 1930 either in NJ or CT.[99] She married FRED ANDERSON about 1911. Fred was born about 1888 in NJ.[100] His death date is unknown. After Elfrieda's death, this family seems to have lost touch with their Vogelbach relatives.

The children of Elfrieda Vogelbach and Fred Anderson are: [101]

26. i. FREDERICK[3] ANDERSON was born in 1912 in NJ.

27. ii. EDMUND ANDERSON was born in 1913 in NJ.

28. iii. ELFRIEDA "BIRDIE" MARGUERETTE ANDERSON was born in 1915 in NJ.

14. viii OSCAR[2] VOGELBACH was born 25 Jan 1897 in Montgomery, NY,[102] and died 27 Dec 1959 in Montgomery, NY.[103] Oscar was an engineer his whole working life. He married ELEANOR WOODS LINDSAY on 6 Mar 1918 in the Knox Presbyterian Church, Kearny, NJ.[104] Eleanor was born 26 Feb 1899 in Kearny, NJ. Her death was 2 Dec 1983 in Thompson Ridge, NY.[105]

---

[96] Social Security Death Index, Ancestry.com, Helen Eckel.

[97] Social Security Death Index, Ancestry.com, William Eckel.

[98] Adolph Vogelbach Household, 1900 Census, *op.cit.*

[99] Fred Anderson Household 1930 census, CT, Fairfield County, Greenwich, ED 139, Sheet 4B, Frieda had died before 1930, and Fred was remarried. Frieda's children, Fred's new wife Mary and her children, plus two servants are in the home that Fred owned at 99 River Side Ave.

[100] Fred Anderson Household, 1920 Census, NJ, Bergen County, Lyndhurst, ED 185, Sheet 16A.

[101] Fred Anderson Household, 1920 Census, *op.cit.* is the source of children's names and years of birth.

[102] Record of Birth for Oscar Vogelbach, NYS Dept of Health Certif# D131535.

[103] Oscar died 27 Dec 1959, according to his death certificate, which is in the collection of Charles Roebuck.

[104] Marriage Certificate for Oscar Vogelbach & Eleanor Lindsay, Dept of Health, Town of Kearny, Hudson County, NJ, Oscar Vogelbach, 21, married Eleanor Woods Lindsay, 19, on 6 Mar 1918. Officiating was Rev. Robert T. Graham in the Knox Presbyterian Church.

[105] Social Security Death Index at Ancestry.com and death certificate in the collection of Charles Roebuck.

The children of Oscar Vogelbach and Eleanor Woods Lindsay are:

29. i. ELEANOR[3] VOGELBACH was born 25 Dec 1919 and died in Aug 1925.[106]

30. ii. ETHEL VOGELBACH was born 10 May 1922 in NJ and died 12 Jul 2006 in Goshen, NY.[107] She married CHARLES ROEBUCK in 1946. Charles was born 29 Oct 1921 and died 19 June 1988 in NY.[108] Ethel and Charles had two children.

31. iii. ROBERT VOGELBACH was born 11 Nov 1923. He died 26 Sep 1992 in Thompson Ridge, Orange County, NY.[109] He married JEAN THOMPSON in 1951. Jean was born 19 Feb 1925 and died 15 Oct 1997 in Thompson Ridge, Orange County, NY.[110] Robert and Jean had three children.

32. iv. LIVING VOGELBACH married WALTER ROEBUCK. Walter was born 12 Feb 1931 and died 20 Jan 1996 in Montgomery, Orange County, NY.[111] They had three children.

33. v. THEODORE OSCAR VOGELBACH was born 18 May 1935 and died 10 Aug 2003 in Monroe, Amherst County, VA.[112] He and his wife, who is living, had three children.

15. ix. EDMUND ADOLPH[2] VOGELBACH born on 21 March 1899[113] and died in CT between 1925-1930.[114] He worked for F. Schumacher & Co., NYC.[115] Edmund married PHYLLIS BECK about 1924, and they had one child. After Edmund died, his wife Phyllis married a man named NOBLE ARMSTRONG, and Noble adopted Phyllis' daughter.[116] Phyllis was born 25 March 1897 and died Oct 1969 in Los Angeles, CA.[117]

---

[106] Note from Charles Roebuck, June 2009.
[107] Social Security Death Index on Acestry.com.
[108] Social Security Death Index on Acestry.com.
[109] Social Security Death Index on Acestry.com.
[110] Social Security Death Index on Acestry.com.
[111] Social Security Death Index on Acestry.com.
[112] Social Security Death Index on Acestry.com.
[113] WW I Draft Registration Card for Edmund Adolph Vogelbach, Ser No 783, Order No A-2986, on Ancestry.com, and Adolph Vogelbach Household, 1900 Census, NY Orange County, Crawford, ED 5 Sheet1A.
[114] Phyllis Vogelbach Household, 1930 census, CT, Fairfield County, Ridgefield, ED 173, Sheet 10B. Phyllis is a widow by 1930. Edmund was listed in the 1925 Manhattan Directory.
[115] WW I Draft Registration Card for Edmund Adolph Vogelbach, *op.cit.*, and 1925 Manhattan Directory, Edmund Vogelbach, clerk F. Schumacher & Co.
[116] Source: Charles Roebuck.
[117] Social Security Death Index at Ancestry.com.

The only child of Edmund Vogelbach and Phyllis Beck is:

34. i.   ELIZABETH[3] VOGELBACH, born about 1925.

16. x.   FANNY[2] VOGELBACH was born 15 Sept 1903 in New York and died in May 1984 in Southbury, CT.[118] She married MYRON LEWIS about 1924.[119] Myron was born 9 July 1900, and he died 10 Dec 1990 in Waterbury, CT.[120] The Lewis's are an old Southbury family going back to the 1700s, at least. All of Fanny and Myron's seven children were born and raised in Southbury. Myron worked as an insurance agent[121] and then a milling machine operator.[122]

Children of Fanny Vogelbach and Myron Lewis are:

35. i.   LIVING[3] LEWIS and his wife have three children.

36. ii.   LIVING LEWIS married ALFRED JURGENS in 1949. Alfred was born in 1925 and died in 2001. They had two children.

37. iii.   LIVING LEWIS married LEONA BRYANT in 1958. Leona was born in 1934 and died in 1984. They had five children.

38. iv.   LIVING LEWIS

39. v.   ROBERT EDMUND LEWIS was born 4 May 1930 and died 12 June 1998.[123] He was a carpenter in general construction. He had two children with his first wife. After they divorced, Robert remarried. His second wife has two children from her previous marriage.

40. vi.   LIVING LEWIS married ROBERT WILLIAM CHAPMAN in 1959. Robert was born 14 Aug 1932 and died 8 June 2000 in Southbury, New Haven County, CT.[124] They had two children.

41. vii. LIVING LEWIS and her husband have three children.

---

[118] Social Security Death Index at Ancestry.com.

[119] Myron Lewis Household, 1930 Census, CT, New Haven County, Town of Southbury, ED 5-196, Sheet 10A, says Myron was 24 and Fanny was 21 when they married. The census record says Myron was born in CT about 1900, and he was an insurance agent.

[120] Connecticut Death Index, Ancestry.com, Certif 27553, provides Myron's birth and death information.

[121] Myron Lewis Household, 1930 census, CT, *op. cit.*

[122] Connecticut Death Index at Ancestry.com. Myron Lewis death certif# 27553.

[123] Connecticut Death Index, Ancestry.com, Certif 14282, provides Robert's birth, death, and occupation.

[124] Social Security Death Index at Ancestry.com provided Robert Chapman's birth and death information.

Chapter 3

John VOGELBACH 1862-1947
Fanny MORITZ 1866-1927

Photos of John Vogelbach and Fanny Moritz, circa.1886, perhaps at the time of their marriage.
From the collection of Peter Heidtmann.

John Vogelbach said he once lived on a little farm in Switzerland with goats, like Heidi's grandfather.[1] He was the son of Anton Vogelbach and Elisabeth Schneebeli, and was born in 1862[2,3] in a town called Küsnacht,[4] a few miles south of Zürich, Switzerland on the eastern shore of Lake Zürich. The sunsets in the west over the lake must have been very beautiful!

---

[1] John told this story to his granddaughter Grace Vogelbach.

[2] John Vogelbach Household, 1900 Census, NY, Orange County, Town of Montgomery, ED 28, Sheet 13A, says John was born Apr 1862 in Switzerland.

[3] Cemetery Record at Friends Cemetery for John Vogelbach, Westbury NY, says John's birthday was 24 April.

[4] Certificate of Marriage for Fanny Moritz and John Vogelbach, 21 Nov 1886, Health Dept, City of NY, certif# 65933, spells the town Küssnacht, but that town was much farther from Zurich where the family registered all their births. Küsnacht is John's more likely birthplace.

Religion

John grew up in a strict Catholic home. Peter Heidtmann learned from his mother Martha "that John came from a strict Catholic family, but that he rebelled against the religion of his parents while he was still a boy or a young man in Switzerland. She thought that this disaffection from his family was at least a part of the reason for his immigration to the States." Grace Vogelbach remembers a slightly different story: "Grandpa John Vogelbach was Catholic when he came over here, but changed when he heard people coming out of the church talking about other people."

Immigration

John left Switzerland in 1882 when he was about 20 years of age[5] and arrived in New York to be greeted warmly by his older brother Adolph who was already in the United States. The two men and their extended families remained close for their entire lives. They probably lived together for a few months, or even a year, after John immigrated and until Adolph married in 1883. John found work in Manhattan in his trade as a home carpenter and stairbuilder, and soon had a good reason to save some money. He had met the young and very refined and loving Fanny Moritz.[6] Fanny was a few years younger than John and had recently come to the United States with her brother and sister after their parents both died.[7] Fanny, too, was Swiss; her birthplace was a town called Thalwil on the opposite shore of Lake Zürich from John's hometown.

Young Married Life

About a year after John and Fanny met, they were married. Their marriage took place on a clear, crisp November day, the Sunday before Thanksgiving in 1886. They may had been living together right before they married, because the address on their marriage certificate is the same for both of them.[8]

John and Fanny lived in Manhattan in the early years of their marriage. Several close relatives also lived in Manhattan at this time, and they were all in either walking distance or easy commuting distance: John's brother Adolph and his wife Barbara ,[9] and Fanny's brother

---

[5] John Vogelbach Household, 1900 census, *op.cit.* The census record says he had resided in NY State for the last 18 years, so 1882 is year of John's immigration.

[6] Swiss Archives, Ansässenverzeichnis von Thalwil (E III 121.19), Amalie Fanny, born 5 April 1866, Thalwil.

[7] Passenger List, S.S.France, General Transatlantic Company, page 2 and 5, Ancestry.com. S.S.France set out from LeHavre and arrived in New York Harbor 28 Feb 1884.

[8] Certificate of Marriage for Fanny Moritz and John Vogelbach, *op.cit,* 21 Nov 1886. Residence was 429 East 81st Street. The minister lived on E 83rd St. The church was probably Immanuel Evangelical Lutheran on 88th and Lexington Ave. John's occupation was stairbuilder. A NYTimes article called "The Fine Weather Fills the Roads with Speedy Trotters" describes a cool crisp day on 21 Nov 1886.

[9] Manhattan Marriage Register, 23 Dec 1883, Adolph Vogelbach and Barbara Hassler, 1420 Ave.A, Lower East Side

Jacob and their sister Bertha, both still single,[10,11] and Fanny's married sister Marie Moritz Seitz and her family.[12]   When Fanny's first child Otto was born in 1887, there were many relatives who probably came to celebrate Otto's birth, and later his baptism.[13]   Maybe little Fanny and Helen Seitz were allowed to play with their baby cousin, change his diapers, and feed him whenever they visited the Vogelbach Family.

The family attended a German Lutheran Church when they lived in Manhattan. Participating in services with German speaking neighbors helped them feel comfortable in their new surroundings. Given John's disaffection for the Catholic Church, attending a Lutheran congregation would feel familiar, yet distinct enough from Catholicism, to satisfy him. Otto was baptized in the Lutheran Church on 88th Street and Lexington Avenue. Grace Murphy, John's great-great granddaughter, who lived in that neighborhood in the late 1990s, said the church is still serving the Upper East Side. Otto's godmother was his Aunt Bertha Moritz, still unmarried, and his godfather was a man named Andreas Scholler. Otto seems to have gotten his middle name from this man. A guess about the Scholler's connection to the Vogelbachs is that he was a special friend of the family or maybe an in-law, but so far, his exact connection is unknown.[14]

Naturalization

While they lived in Manhattan, John decided to begin the process of becoming a naturalized citizen. He submitted his "papers" swearing his intention to complete the process.[15]   Over the next few years he had to learn to read and write English. By 1892, he was ready; then he had to pass a civics test, renounce his allegiance to Switzerland, and swear new allegiance to the United States of America.[16]   This is a very emotional experience for most immigrants. We can imagine John and Fanny inviting all their Vogelbach and Moritz in-laws to have a big celebration for John. This may have inspired John's brother-in-law Jacob Moritz to become naturalized, too. Jacob became a citizen in 1894.[17]

---

[10] 1890 NYC Directory, on Ancestry.com. Jacob Moritz lived at 1980 Second Ave nr 102nd St, NYC.

[11] Certificate of Marriage for Jacob Moritz and Lizzie Weiss, 31 Aug 1889, NYC certif. # 9265. Jacob and Lizzie lived at 528 E 84th St., Upper East Side.

[12] Louis Seitz Household, 1900 census, NY, Manhattan, ED 767, Sheet 14B, Marie and Louis Seitz and their family lived at 423 E 83rd St, Manhattan, Upper East Side.

[13] Certificate of Baptism for Otto Vogelbach 22 July 1888, Immanuel Evangelical Lutheran Church at East 88th and Lexington Ave, in the collection of Peter Heidtmann, documents Otto's birth as 9 Oct 1887.

[14] Charles Scholler Household, 1890 NYC Directory, There was a Charles Scholler, stairbuilder, living at 1677 Ave A, which was near Adolph Vogelbach's residence, 1420 Ave A. He may be related to Andrew Scholler in the Andrew Scholler Household, 1900 census, NY, Bronx, District 1043, Sheet 8B, born 1880, carpenter.

[15] John Vogelbach's Declaration of Intention, Superior Court of the City of New York on 14 April 1885. He resided at 421 E 76th Street, Manhattan.

[16] Naturalization Papers for John Vogelbach, 21 Oct 1892, in Queens County Court. Present was Hon. Ganet J. Ganelson, County Judge.

[17] Naturalization Papers for Jacob Moritz, 13 June 1894, NYC Common Pleas Court, Bundle 773, Record 81. Residence was 2093 Madison Ave., near 132nd St.

The Move from Manhattan to Queens

Perhaps in search of a better job, John, Fanny, and baby Otto moved to Corona in Flushing, Queens. Two more children were born there: Joseph in 1889 and Louis in 1891.[18] Grace Vogelbach remembered visiting the neighborhood with her parents when she was young. Joseph wanted to show his own young family where he was born. Grace said there was a large lake in the neighborhood; it was probably Meadow Lake in Flushing Meadows Park which is now famous as the site of the 1964 Flushing World's Fair, Citi Field, NY Hall of Science, Queens Museum of Art, , the Unisphere, and the USTA National Tennis Center.

As a self-employed carpenter, John was part of a network of skilled workers in the building trade. He must have had to find work in a variety of ways. Apparently, he was not part of a union, so he had no union representative sending him to a waiting employer. He must have had to rely heavily on word-of mouth. One worker probably alerted his friends that a construction job was opening up, and they would all find their way to the site to apply for work. John used public transportation to get to work. Perhaps he rode the horse drawn "omnibus" or the trolley that ran along Roosevelt Ave.

For seventy years trolleys ran in all five boroughs of New York City. Trolleys operated by electrical power delivered through wires running overhead or in underground conduits. They were faster and cleaner than horsecars.[19]

Then To a Farm in Montgomery, NY

In about 1894, with three little children and another baby on the way, John and Fanny rented a farm in Orange County, NY,[20] a few hours north of Manhattan. Three of John and Fanny's daughters were born in Montgomery or the adjoining Town of Crawford: Olga in 1894, Rosella in 1897, and Fanny in 1899. Orange County may have reminded John of his childhood in Switzerland on a farm with goats. John's brother Adolph had already moved up to this hilly, rural area to be close to his wife's family for a while. Adolph had bought a farm in Crawford.[21] Other family members and in-laws owned farms in the area as well; some of

---

[18] Certificate of Baptism for Joseph Vogelbach, in the collection of Veronica Black, states that Joseph was born in Corona on 23 Aug 1889.

Social Security Application for Louis Vogelbach, #070-03-8203, said Louis was born on April 8, 1891 in Flushing NY. This was probably Corona, Flushing, where his brother Joseph was born.

[19] NYC's Transit Museum website: http://www.transitmuseumeducation.org/trc/background The trolleys operated from around 1880 to about 1950.

[20] John Vogelbach Household, 1900 census, *op.cit.* The family was enumerated in Montgomery Town, Orange County, NY where they rented a farm, which was #202 on the farm schedule.

[21] Adolph Vogelbach Household, 1900 census, Orange County, Crawford Town, ED 5, Sheet 1A. Adolph owned a farm, with a mortgage, which was #009 on the farm schedule.

these farms were quite large. A few Vogelbach relatives still live on farms in Orange County.[22] John did not actually do much farming there; rather, he worked as a stairbuilder in various farm houses nearby.

John passed his woodworking skills down to his son Joseph, who was an enthusiastic apprentice. Joseph drew heavily on his father's coaching later in life when he built his own home in Holbrook, and when he made many beautifully carved pieces of furniture for his home. Joseph's basement in Holbrook was filled with the old woodworking tools that his father had willed to him. (During visits to my grandfather's house, I would often stand in front of the workbench and finger the tools, wondering what each might be used for.) Some tools were utilitarian, and some were needed just for decorative work. After Joseph died, John's great-grandsons were given a few of these tools.

When Grace Vogelbach was young, her father Joseph took the family to visit a farm in Kerhonkson, NY, in the Catskills about 20 miles north of Middletown. Joseph told Grace that he remembered sleeping in haylofts when his father worked on farms upstate. Joseph said he remembered watching rats run through the hayloft; this always stuck in Grace's mind, and she passed this image down to us. Living on a farm in a rural area did not work out very well for John and Fanny, so the family moved back to Queens. Actually, farming did not work out well for John's brother Adolph, either, because he also decided to move back to an urban area shortly after John did.

The Return to Queens (ca.1903 to ca.1919)

After the short stint on the farm, John moved his family to Jamaica, Queens, which was a few miles south and east of their old neighborhood in Flushing. One of John's nephews, Robert, lived in Jamaica, too, around this time.[23] Before modern days, it was very common for families to live near relatives, unlike today, when cousins and siblings are spread all over the country, even all over the world.

John and Fanny's last two children, Adolph and Martha, were born in Jamaica.[24] About twenty years separated the births of their oldest, Otto, and youngest child, Martha.

Peter Heidtmann wrote: "Martha Vogelbach's birth certificate confirms that she was born in Jamaica. At that time (28 March 1907) her mother (Fanny Vogelbach) was 41 years old. Her certificate also indicates that Fanny had 12 previous children. This establishes

---

[22] Charles Roebuck and his Aunt Barbara Roebuck still live in Orange County near the old Vogelbach and Hassler farms.

[23] Robert Vogelbach Household, 1910 census, NY, Queens, Jamaica, ED 1255, Sheet 13B. John and his first cousin Robert and his wife Frieda lived in walking distance from each other.

[24] Birth Certificate for Martha Vogelbach, NYS Dept of Health, Certif # 1698, 28 March 1907, residence was 508 South Street, Jamaica, NY. Eight of Fanny's thirteen children were alive in 1907. In a conversation with the author, Eileen Wylie said she believed her Uncle Adolph (b. 21 Dec 1903) was born in Jamaica.

something my mother always claimed, that she was the last of 13 children. Previously I had wondered whether some of her mother's earlier pregnancies might have resulted in miscarriages or stillbirths. Clearly this is not the case. Fanny Moritz Vogelbach had five babies who died either in infancy or childhood. My mother knew none of their names, as she told me when I asked her about this many years ago."

John and Fanny seem to have waited until this time to have some of their children baptized. For example, we know that Joseph and Rosella were not baptized until the family was back in Queens. Joseph's Baptismal Certificate says he was baptized in 1904 in the German Lutheran Church called St Paul's in Jamaica, Queens.[25] Rosella's Certificate says she was baptized at the same church, but in 1906.[26] Her godparents were her Uncle Adolph and Aunt Barbara Vogelbach.

Around 1910, when little Adolph (Adie) was only four or five, he lost part of a foot in a childhood accident; he was left with only his ankle and heel on one foot. The foot had been crushed between a ferryboat and a landing pier. Olga Jargstorff, also known as Chezi, said that her mother Olga, herself only about age 12, was sent to the hospital to ask how many of her brother's toes had been lost. The doctor told her, "all of them." In spite of this traumatic event, Adie was an avid fisherman throughout his life.

The Children Begin to Go Out on Their Own

Around 1910, the older children of John and Fanny started to leave home to begin their own lives. Otto was already working as a coppersmith,[27] perhaps influenced by his Uncle Adolph Vogelbach, who was a coppersmith. Remember, the John and Adolph Vogelbach families had lived near each other in a few places while Otto was growing up, and maybe Otto watched Adolph at work. Otto seems to have specialized in "tinning," according to his nephew Ronald Vogelbach. "Tinning" meant either dipping iron or steel objects into molten tin or molten silver. "Tinning" could also mean tin-plating or silverplating, an electrical process. Ronald said his Uncle Otto melted silver dimes and quarters to create beautiful household objects and objects d'art.

Otto married Lilly Washing around 1913.[28] A few years after their marriage, the couple moved to Washington, DC. While they were living there, Otto had to register for the World

---

[25] Certificates of Baptism and Confirmation for Joseph Vogelbach. Joseph was baptized and confirmed by Rev Frederick Stoebener on 27 Mar 1904 in St. Paul's German Lutheran Church, 120 Herriman Ave., Jamaica, NY.
[26] Baptismal Certificate for Rosella Vogelbach, as read to the author by Ruth Ritter, says Rosella was baptized on 24 Jun 1906 by Friedrich Stochauser [probably Stoebener] of 120 Herriman Ave., Jamaica,
[27] John Vogelbach Household, 1910 census, NY, Queens, Jamaica, ED 1276, Sheet 15A. Otto was already working as a coppersmith. Little Martha was three years old at the time of the census.
[28] Otto Vogelbach Household, 1920 census, Washington DC, ED-125 Sheet 13A.

War I draft, and he was called up for military service.[29]   The photo
shows Otto in his WW I army uniform; it is in the collection of
Peter Heidtmann.

It is not known how Otto and Lilly met, but the 1930 census tells us
that it was Lilly's second marriage. She was about six years older
than Otto, of Scandinavian descent, though she was born in the US.
The couple first lived in the NW quadrant of Washington DC then
bought a home in the NE quadrant.[30]   They also lived in Arlington,
VA, for a while. Otto and Lilly had no children together, and it is
believed that Lilly had no children from her first marriage either.

Ronald Vogelbach said, "Uncle Otto had done some work for
Woodrow Wilson in the White House. He must have been very
good at what he did because some of his pieces are in the White House Museum."

Joseph Served in the Army Corps of Engineers in Hawaii

Joseph graduated from high school about the same time that Martha was born, and he spent
some time after graduation looking for outdoor work or carpentry. He really liked to work
with his hands and was great at solving woodworking problems.[31]

After a few months of job hunting, he joined the
Army Corps of Engineers and was stationed at Fort
DeRussy, Hawaii with the 2nd Army Battalion.
Joseph joined the Army at age 18 and left the Army
at age 21. His years of service were from 1908 to
1911, [32] luckily not at a time of war. His highest
rank was Corporal. [33]   The photo shows Joseph
Vogelbach, on the right, in Hawaii in 1910, and is
from the collection of Peter Heidtmann.

Fort DeRussy was on the southern tip of the island of Oahu and was one of four forts
established in 1909 for the defense of Honolulu and Pearl Harbor. The Army Corps of
Engineers designed and built these military installations.[34]

---

[29] WW I Draft Registration Card 1917, Ancestry.com, for Otto Andreas Vogelbach, No 2176, Otto's residence
was 1251 22nd NW, Washington DC. Otto was a coppersmith.
[30] Otto Vogelbach Household, 1930 census, Washington D.C., ED 232, Sheet 57A. 122 Otis Street, NE.
[31] Conversation with Grace Vogelbach
[32] Death Certificate for Joseph Vogelbach, NYS Dept of Health, Dist 5154, Registered No. 270.
[33] Joseph Vogelbach's Appointment Certificate, in the collection of Veronica Black. Joseph was appointed
Corporal on 1 Sept 1910 at Fort DeRussy, Honolulu, Territory of Hawaii.
[34] http://www.25idl.army.mil/ArmyMuseumDerussy/my%20webs/museum/images/defending_an_island.htm

When Joseph returned to Jamaica, Queens, he fell in love with Florence Beyers, his future wife. The story is that they met through one of Joseph's sisters, but it was not at high school. None of the Vogelbach sisters attended Florence's commercial high school, Heffley-Brown, a prestigious secretarial school in Brooklyn, so we are not sure how they met Florence. Florence did have an aunt, Amelia Beyer Zahn, who lived in Jamaica on the same street as St. Paul's Lutheran Church, so the Beyers may have known the Vogelbachs from that church. The photo, *circa* 1915, is of Olga, Joseph, and Florence, and is in the collection of the author.

When Joseph told his mother that he wanted to marry Florence, his mother told him, "You better get a steady job," and she filled out an application for him at the New York City Police Academy. Joseph and Florence married on 12 Oct 1915 in Our Lady of Angels Catholic Church. His sister Olga and her fiancé Jules Jargstorff were their witnesses.[35] All during his married life Joseph worked as a policeman,[36] though his true calling was carpentry.

Louis' Love Affair

At this time, Louis was also coming of age. He worked on farms in upstate New York as a farmer and seasonal field laborer. He seems to have spent time with his Uncle Adolph's family in Crawford and at other farms in central New York State. It was in Spencerport, near Rochester, that Louis met Rose Covington, a married woman with a child, and they fell deeply in love. This photo of Louis, *circa* 1910, is from the collection of Peter Heidtmann.

Rose was many years older than Louis, being about forty when they began their great love affair.[37] Rose's brother George owned a fruit farm, which is perhaps where Louis picked apples and met Rose.[38]

---

[35] Certificate of Marriage for Florence Beyer and Joseph Vogelbach, Our Lady of Angels Parish Register, 12 Oct 1915, 7320 Fourth Ave., Brooklyn NY.

[36] Appointment Certificate states that Joseph became a NYC Policeman on 28 Apr 1914. He retired about 1940.

[37] Charles H Covington Household, 1880 census, NY, Orleans County, Kendall, ED 147, Page 32D, Rosa Covington was 7, therefore born ca. 1873. Louis was born in 1891, so there was an 18 year difference in age.

[38] George Covington Household, 1910 Census, NY, Monroe County, Town of Parma, ED29, Sheet 11A.

Martha told her son Peter the following story: "Louis went to work picking apples one season in upstate NY. When he returned to Queens, he had a woman with him. Louis wanted the woman to stay with him, but when Fanny learned that the woman was already married, she said that Rose would have to leave. Louis said that, if Rose could not stay, he would not stay either, and he was true to his word. He left with the woman and was never heard from again."

Beverly Wylie added this element to the sad saga of Louis: "My mother, Fanny, used to tell me that Louis was involved with a divorced woman, which was not considered proper. She said that when she was working in NYC for the Grand Central RR, she received a note from Louis saying he was in the 'Hell's Kitchen' part of Manhattan. Mom never answered the note and this was the last she heard of him."[39]

When Louis left home in 1915, his mother Fanny took it very hard, even though we might think his leaving was partly her own doing. According to Peter Heidtmann, she tried desperately to contact him, and her health deteriorated.

One time, Louis' mother Fanny thought she saw his photograph in a magazine article about the war. She could have sworn it was her son. The photo had a caption that identified the unit; she wrote to the commanding officer, but he wrote back saying he did not recognize the name Louis Vogelbach.

Actually, by then the couple had moved to Albany, New York, and was living at 54 Columbia Street.[40] His WW I draft card says that Louis was unemployed, though his usual employment was "farmer." He wrote on the draft card that he was single, and described himself as "tall, slender, with black hair and dark brown eyes." Though he registered for the draft, Louis was not called up by the Army.[41]

Louis' mother Fanny saved two letters from Spencerport. They are now in the collection of Peter Heidtmann and are transcribed on the following pages. One letter was sent from a woman named Lulu, Rose's sister-in-law, to one of the Vogelbach daughters in 1916. The other letter was written in 1924 on the back of a letter Fanny had mailed in 1920. Here are the texts of these heartbreaking letters with their original spelling and grammar to help the reader "hear" the women themselves. Please refer to the "Covington Family Tree" in the Appendix to see the relationships of the various people mentioned.

The first letter indicates that Rose confided in her sister-in-law Lulu. Lulu wrote the letter to her friend Fanny, Louis' younger sister.

---

[39] Note from Beverly Wylie, 1 Jan 2001, to the author.
[40] WW I Draft Registration Card 1917 for Louis Vogelbach, Ancestry.com.
[41] Louis Vogelbach Household, 1930 census, NY, Broome County, Binghamton, ED 4-21, Sheet 14B.

Spencerport, NY   Jan 11, 1916

Dear Friend,

How are you, Fred is some better, We are again to farm it 4 miles south of Spencerport. It is funny Avery never answered it, because he intended to. Manley is still there, and she is to corners. Hope your mother is well & sister. There is so many sick.

Fred father is very sick with heart trouble very bad - can't hardly talk, He keeps asking for Rose I have wrote to her where she told me to, but know word. Well Fred is waiting to mail this. Write again.

Lulu

The next letter is from Fanny to Rose's mother, Harriet Covington, in Spencerport.[42]

Westbury   13th April/20

My dear Friend,

It is now a year that I heard from you. I sincerely hope that you are well. Have you ever heard any thing concerning your Daughter or Louis. I never heard anything. I saw a picture in a Magazine and I saw a young Man that looked gust like my Son Louis. So I wrote to that Camp to the General. But he wrote back to me telling me that there was no such a Man with that Name. Well he might went under a other Name. But I pretty sure it is the Face of my Son. So I am going to write to the war Dep. to the Adjutant General of the Arme, Wash D.C. asking him that his records be searched for a trace of my son. Will you kindly let me know if you ever heard any thing or if your daughter is home.

We are in Westbury L.I. We bout a house there as the Rent is to high. I hope you are all well. I was very sick this last Winter.

So you know how it feels when you know one of your children is away and you don't know where they are. It is going on 5 Years now and he never wrote a single Word. And when you think how good you was to the

---

[42] Charles H Covington Household, 1920 Census, NY Monroe, Ogden Town, Spencerport Village, ED 27, Sheet 7B. Charles H. 71 and Harriet Covington 67. Charles was the janitor of the public school in Spencerport in 1920. He was a naturalized US citizen who came from England in 1867.

Son. It hurts. Nobody knows but the one who has to go through. Now I hope this finds you well and hope to get a early answer from you.

As ever your Friend,

Fanny Vogelbach   Box (350) Westbury L.I. N.Y.

Mrs. Covington's reply was written on the back of Fanny's letter, a year later.

Spencerport - NY   Feb 26 - 1924

Dear Friend,

Just run a crost your last letter & think I will pen you a few. We are booth sick this Winter have Weak Hearts - so must go slow do not go out atall do hope you & yours is well. Now Dear Have you any good News for us? We do not hear or see any thing & begin to think We never shall & We do need her so verry Bad - her son hase grone up & is Married. Her Husband is the same fathefull man as he allways was, as near to us as our own son.

Pleas ans soon -

Mrs C H Covington Spencerport - N.Y

In Jan 2000, the author looked up the name Covington in Spencerport, NY, curious to see if any of Rose's family might still be living there. There was a Roy Covington in Spencerport. His widow, Lois, answered the author's inquiry. She is Manley Covington's daughter-in-law.

Dear Mrs. Dente,

In regard about Rose Covington, she was the daughter of Mrs. C. H Covington; Lulu was a daughter-in-law. Rose's first husband's name was Van Geisen. Their son was Avery who passed away 4 or 5 yrs ago. All of the Covingtons have passed away except a few great grandchildren who were too young to know about Rose. I am Roy's wife, so all I know is what I was told. At the time of Mrs. C. H. death (early 1930's) they advertised for Rose in regard to the estate. After 5 yrs no response. Sorry I can't be of any further help.

Sincerely,
Lois Covington

The author's first big breakthrough in solving the mystery about what happened to Louis and Rose came after a search of the Social Security database at Ancestry.com. The name Louis Vogelbach was in this database! It contained Louis' Social Security number, his date of birth, and his date and place of death, 4 Aug 1973 in Chenango Bridge, NY. Using Mapquest.com the author located Chenango Bridge near Binghamton. So, Louis had not died in World War I, as many of his siblings had feared. A copy of Louis' original Social Security number application was acquired to verify his parents' names. This was our Louis. What a find![43] The original application also contains a sample of Louis' handwriting.

Now that Louis' date of death was known, the author asked the Binghamton Public Library to search for an obituary for Louis. They were successful in finding the obituary, and they sent the information back in a week.

> "VOGELBACH - Louis Vogelbach, 82, formerly of 21 Fuller Rd., Binghamton, died at 3 p.m. Saturday at the Chenango Bridge Nursing Home. There are no survivors. He was a retired employee of the Truitt Brothers Shoe Co. Funeral and committal services will be held at 8 p.m. Monday at the Hopler Funeral Home, 483 Chenango St. The Rev. Charles L. Murn, pastor of the Immanuel Presbyterian Church will officiate. Burial will be in the Chenango Valley Cemetery. Friends may call at the funeral home Monday 7 to 8 p.m."

The obituary gave us the name of the cemetery where Louis was buried, and the cemeter's phone number was online. A staff member said Louis was buried with his wife, Rose! She had pre-deceased Louis. The cemetery staff also gave us Rose's date of death: Oct 1959.[44] A request to the Binghamton Library for Rose's obituary was also successful:

> "VOGELBACH, Rose M. died 10/20/1959 buried 10/23/1959, 75,[45] formerly of Binghamton, died in Belfast, Maine where she now resides. She is survived by her husband - Louis Vogelbach of Belfast, Maine. She was a former employee of Drybak Corporation, Binghamton. The body will arrive in Binghamton on Thursday morning and will be taken to Hopler Funeral Home - 483 Chenango Street, where friends may call from 2 to 4 and 7 to 9 PM."

It was bitter sweet to learn that the lovers had lived such a long life together. They had evaded detection by family members until their deaths, apparently never knowing the sorrow their disappearance had caused. What a shame that they never reconciled with their families. Rose's son Avery died without ever learning what happened to his mother.

---

[43] Social Security Application for Louis Vogelbach dated 19 Nov 1936, #070-03-8203 Address: R.D. #1, Kirkwood, NY. Employer: Truitt Brothers, Inc., 350 N. Water St., Binghamton, N.Y. Age: 45 Birthday: April 8, 1891 in Flushing, Queens Co., N.Y. Father: John Vogelbach Mother: Fanny Ritter [sic].

[44] Chenango Valley Cemetery Records, state that Louis bought the plot when his wife Rose died in 1959.

[45] Charles Covington Household, 1880 census, *op.cit.* Referring to information in this source again, Rose was really 86 when she died, contrary to what the obituary says.

During their lifetime, Louis and Rose were factory workers. From 1920 to at least 1939, they worked in Binghamton, New York, at the Truitt Brothers Shoe factory. At first Louis was a leather cutter, and then he became a foreman at the factory.[46, 47] Rose started out making shoe sole veneers but then got a better job as a seamstress[48] in a Binghamton men's clothing factory called Drybak Corp. The author found a photo on E-bay of "a rare vintage hunting jacket" made at Drybak Corp, Binghamton, NY, selling for $475 in the year 2007. Apparently, Drybak produced pieces of high quality clothing that are now collector's items.

Sometime before 1959, Louis and Rose moved to Belfast, Maine, perhaps to retire.[49] Nothing more is known about their life in Maine or New York, except that Louis died alone in the Chenango Bridge Nursing Home in 1973.[50]

Olga Marries the handsome Jules Jargstorff

Olga Vogelbach was the next to leave home. She met a handsome man named Julius "Jules" Jargstorff who lived near the Vogelbach family in Jamaica, Queens. He was tall and slender with blue eyes and light brown hair.[51] Julius attended New York University[52] and was educated as a civil engineer. He did not join the Army Corps of Engineers as Joseph did. Instead, he worked as a civilian, first as a draftsman for the New York Central Railroad, then in the Newburgh shipyard where military ships were built, and then in bridge construction. The country was about to enter World War I, and men had to register for the draft. Jules registered but was not called up for Army service, probably because of his work in the Newburgh shipyard. Luckily, Olga was not left alone during the war, a fate which many other newly married women

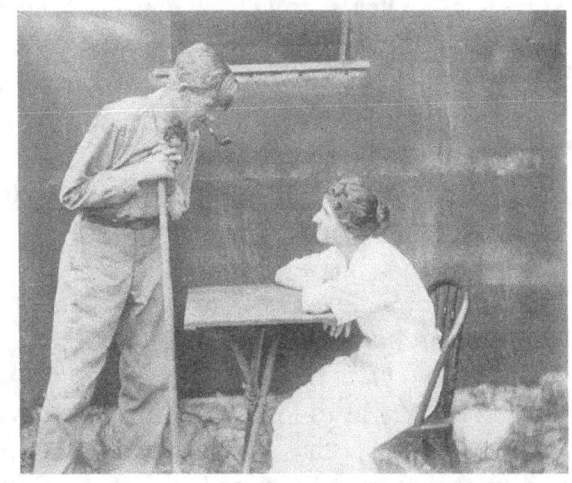

suffered in 1917. The photo, in the collection of their daughter Chezi, was probably taken in Fort Montgomery, New York, in the 1920s.

[46] Louis Vogelbach Household, 1920 census, NY, Broome County, Binghamton, ED 25, Sheet 12A.

[47] 1939 Binghamton City Directory: Vogelbach, Louis (Rose) foreman Truitt Bros., residence 5 Cary Street.

[48] Louis Vogelbach Household, 1930 census, NY, Broome County, Binghamton, ED 4-21, Sheet 14B. Rose was a stitcher of men's wear (probably Drybak, as mentioned in her obituary)

[49] Obituary for Rose VOGELBACH.

[50] Coincidentally, Louis died on August 4, which is the author's birthday.

[51] World War I Draft Registration Card for Julius Jargstorff, dated 5 June 1917, gives us his physical description, his birthday 20 Jan 1891, Darmstadt, IL, and occupation, "draftsman for the NY Central RR."

[52] Conversation between the author and Julius' daughter Olga, also known as Chezi.

The couple married on 16 Sep 1917, probably in Jamaica, Queens. They moved to upstate New York to follow the interesting jobs Julius secured in construction.[53] Chezi said he worked for the government building the Bear Mountain Bridge (opened 1924) and for a little while on the George Washington Bridge (opened 1931). In 1930, Olga and Jules lived in Kingston, but it is not known what project he worked on at that time. It was not the Kingston-Rhinecliff Bridge because that was not begun until much later (1957).[54]

Think about Jules Jargstorff the next time you drive across these bridges, and tell your children that one of your relatives helped to build bridges over the Hudson River!

Ruth Ritter visited her "Aunt Olgie[55] and Uncle Julie" in Fort Montgomery while Jules was working on the Bear Mountain Bridge. She recalled lovely memories of the visit, like drawing water from a well in the woods with her Aunt and Uncle, and enjoying the beautiful sunflowers in the neighborhood. Ruth said her Uncle Julie was a very good swimmer, and she remembers holding on to his back while they swam in a lake. Olga and Jules probably had visits from other close relatives, too, because Jules' brother Theodore and his young family lived in the general area in the 1920s and 1930s. Theodore was a government surveyor.[56] Olga's Vogelbach cousins lived a few miles west in Orange County, so they may have visited sometimes, too.

Olga was a rather shy person. Her daughter said she enjoyed cooking, always had a little kitchen vegetable garden, and liked to read. She was a devoted letter writer with her daughter, no matter where each of them lived. Olga made several patchwork quilts, and crocheted a few afghans.

Olga and Jules moved back to Long Island in the early 1930s - first to Shelter Island. Jules did some preliminary work for a proposed bridge from Shelter Island to Greenport which was intended to replace the ferry, but the project was aborted because of the Great Depression. After that, they lived for a while on Taylor Avenue with Olga's widowed father John and with her sister Martha. This was before Martha was married. After Martha married, Olga and Jules moved to Farmingdale. In the 1940s they moved back to Westbury near John's home, and finally to Indiana. Jules died at their home in Indiana, and Olga lived alone there for a while. When it became apparent that she needed assistance, she moved back east and lived with her daughter. Olga died in a highly regarded nursing home in Brooklyn run by the Catholic Church called Madonna Residence.

---

[53] Jules Jargstorff Household, 1920 census, NY, Orange County, City of Newburgh, ED 147, Sheet 2A, says Jules Jargstorff, 28, was working as a civil engineer.

[54] The bridge opening dates are from the NYS Bridge Authority, http://www.nysba.state.ny.us/Index.html

[55] Email from Chezi on 29 May 2009 says, though, "My mother's nickname was Ogie (pronounced with a long O, and a name I disliked).

[56] Theodore Jargstorff Household, 1930 census, NY, Orange County, Highland Falls, ED 21, Sheet 13A, They lived at 172 Main Street.

Jules' daughter Chezi told the author about her fond memories of her father. "My father began speaking German with me when I first began to talk. He told me bedtime stories in German and taught me folk songs. I spoke German with him regularly until World War II made speaking German very unpopular. I now regret this as, while my German is quite good, it would be much better if I had continued. My father was a great story teller with a wonderful memory. He could recall poetry and bits from Shakespeare which he had learned many years before. His good memory probably had something to do with his being able to learn a bit of American Sign Language so that he was able to communicate with my cousin Junior Ritter who was deaf."[57]

Ruth Ritter said her Uncle Julie and Cousin Olga spoke in German when they did not want Aunt Olga to know what they were talking about, though Chezi said, "My mother didn't speak German but had a pretty good understanding." Ruth mentioned that the Jargstorff Family had a dog named Mudgie. Chezi explained the dog's name this way: "The dog my parents had in Fort Montgomery had a name I can't spell, as it is a Russian word which I can't find in either the dictionary or encyclopedia. My best guess is Mudjik, which they changed to Mudgie (u pronounced as the *ou* in would). The Russian word is the name of a class of people. I'm not sure whether they were peasants, serfs or what. I think that my parents got the name from a man who lived in the area and had supposedly been in the Arctic with dogs and sleds."

Chezi said her father also worked as the Chief Purchasing Officer for the Continental Baking Company. This is the company known for Wonder Bread and Hostess Twinkies. It was a very large corporation with offices in New York City.

Rosella and Frederick John Ritter

Rosella seems to have been a tom-boy as a young woman. Her daughter Ruth says the first time her parents met, Rosella was climbing a tree.

Rosella graduated from Jamaica High School and worked as a seamstress on Fifth Avenue in Manhattan for a while. She was twenty when she married her handsome first cousin Frederick John Ritter. This photo was taken at their wedding, either 1917 or 1918, and is in the collection of Ruth Ritter. Rosella and Fred's mothers were sisters, but the two families did not visit each other very often

---

[57] E-mail to the author dated 28 Nov 2000.

because the Ritters lived in the Bronx, which made it difficult for them to visit the Vogelbachs in Jamaica, Queens. Rosella's sweetness and Fred's charm must have been powerful attractions for the cousins when they did see each other, though.

Fred had spent four years in the US Navy before World War I,[58] having joined when he was only seventeen. His daughter Ruth said he was a boxer during his service. He probably would have made a career out of the Navy, she said, but, "Mother said she would only marry him if he gave up the Navy, which he did."

In their early married life, they lived in an unheated summer bungalow in Netcong, NJ, (off Rte 80 in Morris County). To get water, Rosella had to cut through the ice in Lake Musconetcong. She was very lonesome because few people lived in Netcong during the winter back then. She became pregnant while living in pretty primitive conditions there, and she may have returned to New York to give birth to her son.[59] Fred worked on a railroad that came through Netcong. At the time of the 1920 census, he was working as a brakeman on the DL&W Railroad.[60] Fred later entered a career designing fire engines.

Perhaps Rosella and her five-month old baby, who was always called Junior, needed a break from the severe winter weather, because we find them enumerated with John and Fanny in Westbury in January 1920, without her husband.[61] We can guess that Fred's work kept him in New Jersey, and that is why he was not with Rosella and Junior in Westbury. Instead, he was enumerated in New Jersey, and his mother Bertha Ritter was enumerated with him.

A few years later, the Ritters returned to Queens. When Rosella's mother Fanny died in 1927, the Ritters lived in Westbury to help take care of John Vogelbach. They attended Advent Episcopal Church in Westbury for a while. Joe and Fanny Wylie were Ruth's godparents in that church. Ruth said she attended six months of first grade in Westbury before they moved back to Queens. Even after that, the Ritters went out to Westbury every weekend to play cards with Grandpa John and many of their other relatives. The Ritters attended two other churches, an Evangelical (Lutheran) Church in Queens and then joined a Christian Science Reading Room "because of a friend." Both Fred and Rosella became Readers in the church. Ruth said Olga and Jules sometimes attended the Christian Science church with the Ritters when there was a lecture that sounded interesting to them.

---

[58] World War I Draft Registration Card for Frederick Ritter, dated 5 June 1917, says he already had four years service in the US Navy as a Corpsman, and was then a civilian working in Landing NJ as an electrician.

[59] John Vogelbach Household, 1920 census, NY, Nassau, Hempstead, ED 17, sheet 24B. Julius, 5 months old, born in New York.

[60] Fred Ritter Household, 1920 census, NJ, Morris County, Roxbury Township, Village of Landing, ED 52, Sheet 4A. Landing is about 2.5 miles east of Netcong. Residence: an apartment on Main Road, Landing.

[61] John Vogelbach Household, 1920 census, *op.cit,* Enumerated together at Maple Ave [really Taylor Ave.] are John, Fanny, Fanny, Adolph, Martha, Rosella and baby Julius.

Olga said Aunt Rose usually wore a sweater because she always seemed to feel chilly, and her family took care of Rose's son Junior for a while in the early 1920's when Rosella wasn't feeling well.

Rosella was known for her beautiful sewing. Her early experience on 5th Avenue as a seamstress provided her with skills for a lifetime. She made many doll clothes for her granddaughter Linda, who always had a nice coat for each doll from material left over from her own coats. Rosella was sewing a pair of slacks the night before she died at age 85. Rose and Fred are buried together in Long Island National Cemetery, Pinelawn.[62]

John, Fanny, Young Fanny, Adolph, and Martha in Westbury   1919 to 1947

Peter Heidtmann suggested that Fanny's mental health began to suffer after her son Louis left home and disappeared.

"The move to Westbury, as Martha told the story, took place in 1919. Fanny knew a woman in Jamaica who had a friend in Westbury who knew of a house for sale on Taylor Avenue near Roosevelt Field. Fanny then borrowed some money from a saloonkeeper she knew and went out to Westbury on the train with her friend. Satisfied with the house and its location,[63] she used the borrowed money for a down payment and returned that evening to tell John (her husband). In her letter to Mrs. Covington, Fanny mentions that they moved to the house in Westbury because it cost less than renting in Queens. This was undoubtedly true, but it's my guess that John consented to the move at least in part for the sake of Fanny's mental health. They both may have hoped that a change in locale would be beneficial. In any case, moving day came. Martha and her mother traveled by train to Westbury, and they walked first, carrying suitcases, to the house of the woman who had known about the place on Taylor

---

[62] Burials data found at: http://files.usgwarchives.org/ny/suffolk/cemeteries/babylon/longisland/r/r-14.txt

[63] John Vogelbach Household, 1920 federal census, NY, Nassau, Town of Hempstead, ED 17, Sheet 24B, The family was enumerated on Maple Avenue near Old Country Road, though their residence was really on Taylor Avenue, one house from the corner of Maple Street. Peter Heidtmann sheds light on this mystery: "... the Taylor Avenue house was just one house removed from a corner, and Maple Street was the name of the intersecting road. It could very well be that in 1920 there was yet no other house built next to ours, and the census-taker simply wrote down the wrong street name, calling it Maple Avenue instead of Taylor Avenue."

Avenue. There they had coffee and cake before walking on to their new home, where they were joined later in the day by John, Martha's sister Fanny, and her brother Adolph.

"The move to Westbury unfortunately did not help Fanny. Martha had to quit school after the eighth grade to help her ailing mother at home. Even before that she stayed home from school on the weekly washday. She and her mother used a washboard and washed the clothes at a big tub set up in the kitchen. Martha fondly remembered having lunch--coffee and sandwiches--with her mother, both of them sitting in chairs beside the washtub. In fact, all of Martha's memories of Fanny (apart from her illness) were good."

Fanny had lived a very hard life, and it is not surprising that she had poor mental health in her later years. The mind could go on any woman whose parents died and left her orphaned at a young age, who had to immigrate to America to survive, who moved around a great deal as a young married woman, who lived hand to mouth for many years with small children, who suffered the death of five of her children, and had a son who vanished as a young man.

The three youngest children, Fanny, Adolph, and Martha, settled in to their new home in Westbury and made friends with people in the neighborhood. John himself had a coterie of friends from the building and banking industries in town.

Fanny and Joe Wylie

Young Fanny met Joseph Wylie, her future husband, soon after the move to Westbury, and they married in 1921. They made Westbury their home for most of their married lives. All three of their children were born prematurely at seven months, said her son Joe; people did not even realize she was pregnant. The photo is of Fanny, *circa* 1920, in the collection of Peter Heidtmann.

Fanny and Joe had a cozy home at 140 Asbury Ave, near the Northern State Parkway. The author's family often visited Aunt Fanny and Uncle Joe there; it was an easy ride to Westbury from their home in Plainview. The oldest Doheny girls have many fond memories of Aunt Fanny's huge backyard with blue and red grapes, a garden with vegetables and flowers, and some chickens, rabbits, and even turkeys. Fanny's son Joe said he remembers the unpleasant task of chopping off the birds' heads and plucking them before his mother made wonderful meals out of them. He said they also staked out a rough tennis court in their yard and built a backstop so loose balls would not fly into the street. Fanny made preserves and jellies from their fruit trees and from the grapes in their yard. She was fond of working on hooked rugs and used a wooden frame to support them while she worked.

The author remembers some stuffed hummingbirds and a stuffed squirrel displayed under two glass domes on a cabinet in the living room.[64]

The smell of Joe's pipe smoke usually hung in the air. Joseph was an Irish immigrant from County Tyrone[65] and a great storyteller, as the author remembers him. He had immigrated about 1915 and worked as a carpenter for a contractor in Westbury when his family was young.[66] Later, according to his daughter Eileen, he worked in the railroad industry. He was a clerk, not someone who rode the rails. Joe was tall, and once was asked if he would climb up a church steeple in town to repair it, which he did. He was also in the Hook and Ladder Company of the Westbury Volunteer Fire Department for many years, and served as the Fire Chief for two years. This is a very prestigious position in any Long Island community. The author's family watched Uncle Joe's fire company compete in a training exercise in the 1950s. It was very exciting to see the firemen whizzing around, climbing ladders, and running relays as fast as they could.

This photo is of Joseph Wylie in uniform: "Elected as a member of Hook & Ladder Company No. 1 in January of 1923. Served as Captain of Hook & Ladder in 1926. Elected 2nd Deputy Chief of Department 1953 and 1954; elected First Deputy Chief 1955 and 1956, and, elected Chief of Department in 1956 and 1957." [67]

Fanny and Joe's grandson Kevin describes his grandmother: "What I remember most about my grandmother is her sparkling dark brown eyes!   She was very devoted to her church, Church of the Advent Episcopal Church, where she was a member of the Altar Guild. That group took care of the altar linens and the vessels and got the church ready for the Sunday Service. Grandma enjoyed tatting and quilting. She was a great baker. I loved her pies and cakes, especially an old-fashioned pound cake she made for my birthday every year. Pound cake meant it was made with a pound of butter! She also made something she called 'potato-chip cookies.' They were also made with lots of butter and were very thin and crisp and dotted with nuts. I remember her delicious Sunday Pot Roast dinners. Grandma had an

---

[64] The author remembers being enthralled by the hummingbirds. It was one of those childhood experiences which led to her adult interest in birding.

[65] E-mail from Joseph Wylie: My father was born 3 Dec 1898 in Gorestown, District of Dungannon in County Tyron, Ireland. The S.S. St. Lewis Ship's Passenger List, dated 1 Feb 1916, found online at Ancestry.com: Joseph Wylie, 17, single male, could read and write, occupation was 'joiner,' sailed from Liverpool 22 Jan 1916, and arrived in NY 1 Feb 1916. His next of kin was his uncle, A. Wylie of Ballymackelduff, Moy, County Tyrone, Ireland. A map of Ireland shows all these places in very close proximity to each other, so I am confident that this is our Joe Wylie on the S.S. St. Lewis.

[66] Joseph Wylie Household, 1930 census, NY, Nassau County, Town of Hempstead, Village of Westbury, ED 30-181, Sheet 7A. The family owned its own home at 140 Castle Ave, worth $8,000, and they owned a radio.

[67] Photo and caption were downloaded from http://www.westburyfd.com/Ex_Chiefs.htm and used with the permission of Michael Rice, Westbury Fire Department, phone conversation with him on 15 June 2009.

electric washing machine with a wringer she cranked to partially dry her clothes. I'm not sure if the wringer was motorized or hand cranked. Even when she lived in Florida, she had that washing machine." The author's sister Elizabeth said Aunt Fanny was one of the sweetest relatives we knew. Her face beamed with pleasure when she saw us arrive for a visit. She told us stories about how much she loved her brother Joseph Vogelbach, our grandfather, stories about him playing with her when she was a small child.

In the late 1960's, Fanny and Joe moved to Clearwater, Florida. The author's parents visited them there, and it was that visit that convinced Grace and Bernard Doheny to move to Florida once Bernie retired. They all thought the warm weather and the beaches in the area were gorgeous.

Joe died in Clearwater in 1973, so he and Fanny did not enjoy Florida together for very long. After his death, Fanny moved back to LI, and lived with her daughter Eileen's family. When the author lived in Roslyn Heights, Long Island, she kept in regular contact with Aunt Fanny and Eileen and Jim Greenlees, and spent many pleasant afternoons with them.

In 1984, Fanny shared several old Vogelbach family photos with the author's sister Elizabeth. Elizabeth copied them and created customized albums with hand sewn covers. She gave the photo albums to her siblings as very special Christmas presents that year.[68]

Death of Fanny Moritz Vogelbach - 1927

Fanny's mental condition got worse and worse, and she needed more help than the family could give her at home. So at the end of July 1927, John brought her to Kings Park State Hospital in Suffolk County, LI. She was there for only two months before she died.[69] She was 61 years old, and her death certificate says she died of heart disease and hardening of the arteries.[70] Fanny was buried in Friends Cemetery in Westbury, NY.[71] Westbury Friends Cemetery, which is the oldest and one of the most beautiful cemeteries in Nassau County, dates from the 1700s and is dotted with many large old trees.[72]

When Fanny died, John was comforted by having several of his children living nearby. The Wylies lived only a mile and a half away, and the Ritters moved out to Westbury at this time. John's two youngest children, Adolph and Martha, were still living at home with him. Martha, age 20, became his chief caregiver, and remained so for the rest of John's life.

---

[68] Those albums were one of the inspirations that led the author to begin this family history project.

[69] Kings Park State Hospital Registry of Death, Fanny Vogelbach, Registered No. 188, held in the Medical Records Dept of Pilgrim Psychiatric Center, West Brentwood, NY. Fanny died 24 Sept 1927.

[70] Certificate of Death for Fanny Vogelbach, NYS Dept of Health, Division of Vital Statistics, Dist 5111, Registered Number 188, stamped 55727. Her cause of death was chronic myocarditis and arteriosclerosis.

[71] Cemetery Record at Friends Cemetery, 550 Post Ave, Westbury NY. Fanny was interred on 28 Sept 1927.

[72] Richard Panchyk , A History of Westbury, LI,, The History Press, 2007, p 28, available on Google Books.

Martha was very interested in what was happening in Roosevelt Field, which was a few hundred yards behind their house. The photo, in the collection of Peter Heidtmann, is of Martha Vogelbach at Roosevelt Field in her flying outfit, *circa* 1930. Many of the early airplane pilots trained at Roosevelt Field, and Martha was involved in what was happening there. Kevin Greenlees said that his grandaunt Martha once dated a "wing walker" who got her to stand on the wing during at least one flight!

Martha's son Peter said, "My mother flew with many of the early airplane pilots at Roosevelt Field. She was among the crowd who saw Lindbergh take off on his historic solo flight across the Atlantic in 1927. I have a certificate for Martha which identifies her as a member of the Eyewitness Club. This group held annual dinners in Westbury celebrating Lindberg's accomplishment and their memories of it, but I could never talk my mother into attending one of them."

Adolph and Martha Married Doris and Wallace Heidtmann

The Heidtmanns were an important Westbury family in the town's building circles, and John Vogelbach apparently knew them quite well. Wallace Heidtmann Sr. was a building estimator, and he owned one of the largest homes on his block; it was at 270 Asbury Ave.[73] Wallace's children probably had chances to interact with John's children frequently, because two Heidtmanns married two Vogelbachs. Adolph "Adie" Vogelbach married Doris Heidtmann, and Wallace Heidtmann Jr. married Martha Vogelbach.

When Adie was 26 and courting Doris, they both worked as bank clerks in Westbury.[74] She was seven years younger than he was.[75] Their marriage took place on 14 Nov 1931 in Mineola, NY. A few years later, Doris's brother Wallace asked Martha to marry him. Adolph and Martha's families stayed particularly close, of course. This photo of Adolph, *circa* 1930, is from the collection of Peter Heidtmann.

---

[73] Wallace Heidtmann Household, 1930 census, NY, Nassau County, North Hempstead, Westbury, ED 30-181, Sheet 7B. Home was worth $17,000 and the family owned a radio. Many professionals lived on the block.
[74] John Vogelbach Household, 1930 census, NY, Nassau County, Hempstead, Westbury, ED 30-93, Sheet 22B, says Adolph Vogelbach 26, was a bank clerk, and Wallace Heidtmann Household, 1930 census, NY, Nassau County, Hempstead, Westbury, ED 30-181, Sheet 7B, says Doris Heidtmann 19, was a bank clerk.
[75] Social Security Death Index on Ancestry.com says Doris was born on 9 Jun 1910.

Adie worked for Liberty Aircraft Corporation and Republic Aviation Corporation, both in Farmingdale. After he retired, he worked for a while as a supervisor for Hicks Nursery and was assigned to Friends Cemetery. Many members of the Hicks family were buried in this cemetery, and the nursery cared for the cemetery at that time. Many members of the extended Vogelbach family are buried in Friends Cemetery.

Adolph invited his older brother Otto to live with them in Westbury after Otto's wife Lilly died. This was from about 1946 to Otto's death in 1952. "Uncle Ottie" was a great cook and pinochle player, Ronald Vogelbach remembers. Actually, the whole Westbury clan got together on Friday nights to play pinochle. The families kept in great touch with each other. Peter Heidtmann recalls that, "Uncle Ottie visited our house for supper every Monday evening while he lived with the Ivy Avenue Vogelbachs, and I loved him. On those evenings my father, Uncle Ottie, and I played three-handed pinochle at the kitchen table after supper, and those games were a big treat in my young life." Otto died in Westbury on 21 Nov 1952 of liver cancer.[76] Ronald Vogelbach said Otto as a heavy drinker.

Adie and Doris bought a home in Cutchogue on Long Island Sound and lived there for a few years before moving to West Virginia.

When Martha and Wallace Heidtmann married, they lived with John in his Taylor Avenue home. The photo at left is of Martha and Wallace, *circa* 1935, from the collection of Peter Heidtmann.

Peter Heidtmann wrote about his father:

"After graduating from Hicksville HS at the age of 16 (first in his class of five), Wallace wanted to attend MIT, but his High School was so small that it didn't offer all the courses he needed to be admitted. Consequently, he went to night school for a year in the city, while working during the day on *The Brooklyn Eagle*. There he worked on stockmarket reports and in the obituary fileroom. After graduating from MIT in 1928, he was hired by Purdy & Henderson, a small structural engineering firm in Manhattan. The lack of building jobs during the Depression, however, forced the company to let him go at the end of 1932, and for the next five years he picked up work as he could. For a while he worked with the laborers on the Ambrose Clark estate in Old Westbury, where his mother's brother (Uncle Ern, he was always called) had some kind of supervisory position. He also helped his father do carpentry work here and there.

---

[76] Cemetery Record at Friends Cemetery in Westbury NY provides the date and cause of death. Date of death is 11/21/52. Interred 11/24/52. Age 65, 0 months, 12 days which would make his birthday 11/9/1887.

"Then through my Uncle Jules - that is, Julius Jargstorff, Chezi's father - he got a job in 1935 with the Continental Baking Company in NYC. There he worked in the purchasing department, a job which at last gave him a regular paycheck again and enabled him to get married.

"In 1937, the year I (Peter) was born, Purdy and Henderson hired him back, and he stayed with them for the long remainder of his working life. In the 1970's he became the president of the company, and he didn't fully retire until the end of 1983, when he was 76. During all those years, of course, he was a commuter on the LIRR, first from Westbury, then (after moving to East Norwich) from Syosset. Wally was never much of a talker. If you wanted to learn anything about what was going on, you usually had to ask him a specific question."

Grace Vogelbach says her husband Bernard Doheny sometimes met Wally on the LIRR on their way into Manhattan in the morning.

When they felt they were getting old, Wally and Martha moved to Athens, OH and lived near their son Peter. Martha had cared for her own father for many years, and now Peter was returning the favor, so to speak. Wally and Martha, unfortunately, both developed dementia in their old age.

About the Taylor Ave. home: Ronald Vogelbach says that Wally made a bench on the roof of the house, and he remembers watching the races at Roosevelt Field from that vantage point. "As best my memory serves, Roosevelt Field, before it became a trotter and pacer horse track, had both midget and big (Indy equivalent for those times) cars. I am sure this was in the late thirties. There was a two car garage on Grandpa Vogelbach's Taylor Avenue property in Westbury. Wally built a bench on the roof peak, with access via ladders. He also had some type of platform for walking from one end of the bench to the other. The bench, of course, is long gone."

John Vogelbach and his Taylor Avenue home are represented in this painting by his grandson Peter Heidtmann. The work, dated *circa* 1998, is called "Ghost of the Patriarch."

Ruth Ritter said Grandpa John raised pigeons for a while and kept them in a coop behind the garage. He also charged people to park on his property so they could walk over to see the races in Roosevelt Field. Grandpa made her a pair of stilts to play with, and Rosella knew how to use them, too. Ruth remembers riding bikes up Post Ave, a dirt road then, with her mother and Aunt Olga. In Queens, where the roads were all paved, they could roller skate, and she really enjoyed doing that.

Ruth and her husband Red bought the Vogelbach family home from Martha after Martha and Wally moved to East Norwich, and the house stayed in the family for many more years.

John Vogelbach's Last Illnesses and Death - 1947

Peter Heidtmann says,

"John Vogelbach, my grandfather, lived with us when I was young. When he became incontinent and was exhibiting some senile behaviors, my mother felt she could no longer care for him, as well as two small children. He was placed in a nursing home in Hempstead, where I remember visiting him on at least one occasion.

"From John Vogelbach's death certificate and old copies of checks my parents wrote to the nursing homes in which he stayed, I learned he was first placed in the Lyn Nursing Home in Lynbrook, for which the first check is dated July 17, 1946. He was transferred to the Hempstead Nursing Home. The first check to that facility is dated June 3, 1947. The death certificate establishes that John Vogelbach died on Nov. 8, 1947, at the Central Islip State Hospital, where he had resided for 1 month and 13 days. The immediate cause of death is given as arteriosclerosis and heart disease. Under 'other conditions' the attending physician lists senile psychosis, simple deterioration.[77] This information suggests that my grandfather was transferred to the state hospital in Central Islip because the staff at the Hempstead Nursing Home could no longer adequately care for (or perhaps control) him. (Eileen Wylie remembered a story that a nurse was trying to trim John's thick mustache, and he roughly pushed the nurse away.)"

John was buried in Friends Cemetery, Westbury, NY next to his wife Fanny.[78]

---

[77] Certificate of Death for John Vogelbach, NY, Dist 5110, Registered No 465 and Central Islip Psychiatric Center Death Registry, Registered No 465, John Vogelbach died on 8 Nov 1947 at age 85yrs, 6mos, 14 days. He was widowed, had worked as a carpenter, and had spent 1 month and 13 days in CI before his death. The medical attendant was Joseph Papa, MD. John was buried in Friends Cemetery, Westbury, and the Undertaker was William M Donahue, 292 Asbury Ave, Westbury.

[78] Cemetery Record at Friends Cemetery in Westbury NY, John was interred on 10 Nov 1947. The cemetery records also list the people buried with him: his wife Fanny and later his son Otto and daughter Olga. The Wylies are also buried in Friends Cemetery.

Genealogical Summary

2. **JOHN**[1] **VOGELBACH** (*Anton*[4]) was born 24 Apr 1862 in Küsnacht, Switzerland,[79] and died 8 Nov 1947 in Central Islip, NY.[80] He immigrated to the United States about 1882, and was a skilled carpenter.[81] He married **FANNY AMALIE MORITZ** on 21 Nov 1886 in Manhattan, NY.[82] She was the daughter of François Moritz and Julia Emmenecker. Fanny was born 5 Apr 1866 in Thalwil, Switzerland,[83] and died 24 Sep 1927 in Kings Park, NY.[84] Fanny Moritz immigrated on 28 Feb 1884.[85] John and Fanny had thirteen children.[86]

Known children of John Vogelbach and Fanny Moritz are:

17.   i.   OTTO ANDREAS[2] VOGELBACH (*John*[1], *Anton*[4]) was born 9 Nov 1887 in Manhattan, NY[87] and died 21 Nov 1952 in NY[88]. He married LILLY WASHING between 1911 – 1916.[89] Lilly was born about 1883 in Pennsylvania[90] and died about 1946.[91] Otto was a coppersmith.[92] He and Lilly had no children.

---

[79] Certificate of Baptism for Otto Vogelbach, dated 28 Dec 1888, states that John Vogelbach was born in Küssnacht, Republic of Switzerland, though Küsnacht is more likely. Central Islip Psychiatric Center Death Registry, repository of records at Pilgrim Psychiatric Center, W Brentwood, NY sets John's date of birth 24 April 1862.

[80] Cemetery Record at Friends Cemetery in Westbury NY, Date of death is 8 Nov 1947. Interred 10 Nov 1947.

[81] John Vogelbach Household, 1900 Census, NY, Orange County, Town of Montgomery, ED 28, Sheet 13A, says 1882 is year of immigration for John, and he was here 18 years. John Vogelbach Household, 1910 census, NY, Queens, ED 1276, Sheet 15A, says year of John's immigration was 1881. John Vogelbach Household, 1930 census, NY, Nassau County, Hempstead, Westbury, ED 30-93, image 43 of 45 on Ancestry.com, immigration was 1880. Each census says John's occupation is carpenter.

[82] Certificate of Marriage for Fanny Moritz and John Vogelbach, Health Dept, City of NY, certif# 65933.

[83] Swiss Archives, Ansässenverzeichnis von Thalwil (E III 121.19), email said Amalie Fanny was born on 5 April 1866 in Thalwil, daughter of François Moritz and Julia Emmenecker

[84] Kings Park State Hospital Registry of Death for Fanny Vogelbach, Fanny died 24 Sept 1927.

[85] Passenger List - SS France on Ancestry.com, Fanny and Bertha Moritz, 20 and 25, arrived NY 28 Feb 1884.

[86] Birth Certificate for Martha Vogelbach, NYS Dept of Health, Certif # 1698, 28 March 1907, says Fanny had twelve children before Martha.

[87] Certificate of Baptism for Otto Vogelbach: Otto was born on 9 Oct 1887 in Manhattan and he was baptized on 22 July 1888 in the Lutheran church on 88th St and Lexington Ave. His sponsors were Andreas Scholler and Bertha Moritz.

[88] Cemetery Record at Friends Cemetery in Westbury NY says Otto died 11/21/52. Interred 11/24/52.

[89] Otto Vogelbach Household, 1930 census, Washington DC, ED 232, Sheet 57A.

[90] Otto Vogelbach Household, 1920 census, Washington DC, ED 125, Sheet 13A.

[91] Conversation with Ronald Vogelbach. Otto moved in with Ronald's family in 1946 after Lilly died.

[92] Otto Vogelbach Household, 1920 census, *op.cit*, and Otto Vogelbach Household, 1930 census, *op.cit*.

+ **18.** ii.   JOSEPH ANTHONY VOGELBACH was born 23 Aug 1889 in Corona, Flushing, NY[93] and he died 23 Oct 1952 in Holbrook, NY.[94] Joseph married FLORENCE ELIZABETH BEYERS (1887-1960) on 12 Oct 1915 in Brooklyn[95] Joseph was a NYC policeman.[96] Joseph and Florence had five daughters.

19. iii.   LOUIS VOGELBACH was born 8 Apr 1891 in Flushing, NY[97] and died 4 Aug 1973 in Chenango Bridge, NY.[98] His common law wife was ROSE MAY COVINGTON. Rose was born about 1873 in New York[99] and died 20 Oct 1959 in Belfast, Maine.[100] They had no children.

20 iv.   OLGA VOGELBACH was born 2 Dec 1894 in Crawford, Orange County, NY.[101] She died 1 Aug 1984 in Brooklyn, NY and was buried in Westbury Friends Cemetery.[102] She married JULIUS ERNST JARGSTORFF on 16 Sep 1917 in Jamaica, Queens.[103] Julius was born on 20 Jan 1891 in Darmstadt, IL[104] and died on 3 Nov 1977, in Lafayette, IN.[105] He was an engineer.[106] They had one daughter.

21 v.   ROSELLA VOGELBACH was born 29 Aug 1897 in Crawford, Orange County, NY[107] and died 16 Feb 1982 in Westbury, NY.[108] She married FREDERICK JOHN

---

[93] Certificate of Baptism for Joseph Vogelbach, St. Paul's Lutheran Church, Jamaica. Joseph was born on 23 Aug 1889 in Corona, but baptized several years later on 27 May 1904 in Jamaica, NY.

[94] Certificate of Death for Joseph Vogelbach, NYS Dept of Health, District 5154, Registered # 570.

[95] Certificate of Marriage for Florence Beyer and Joseph Vogelbach in the Parish Register of Our Lady of Angels Roman Catholic Church, they lived at 7320 Fourth Ave., Brooklyn.

[96] Certificate of Appointment to the Police Department of the City of New York, 24 Feb 1914, in the collection of Veronica Black, Holbrook, NY.

[97] John Vogelbach Household, 1900 census, NY, Orange County, Town of Montgomery, ED 28, Sheet 13A corroborated by Louis Vogelbach's WWI Draft Registration Card at Ancestry.com, 5 June 1917.

[98] Obituary for Louis Vogelbach, in the obituary file of Broome County Library, Binghamton, NY.

[99] Charles Covington Household, 1880 census, NY, Orleans County, Kendall, ED 147, Page 32D, Rosa Covington was 7, so born ca. 1873.

[100] Obituary for Rose Vogelbach, in the obituary file of Broome County Library, Binghamton, NY.

[101] John Vogelbach Household, 1900 census, *op.cit*, Olga was born Dec 1894 in NY. Olga's daughter Chezi said her mother was born on Dec 2 in the Town of Crawford, NY. Olga was never able to obtain a birth certificate, so the exact place of birth is not documented.

[102] Cemetery Record at Friends Cemetery in Westbury NY, Olga died 1 Aug 1984 in Brooklyn at age 89.

[103] Conversation with his daughter Chezi Jargstorff.

[104] Conversation with his daughter Chezi Jargstorff.

[105] Social Security Records at Ancestry.com, #090-09-6739, Julius was born 20 Jan 1891, and he died Nov 1977 in West Lafayette, Tippecanoe County, Indiana.

[106] Julius Jargstorff Household, 1920 census, NY, Orange County, City of Newburgh, ED 147, Sheet 2A.

[107] John Vogelbach Household, 1900 census, *op.cit*, Rosella was born Aug 1897. Ruth Ritter provided the day and place.

RITTER, the son of Bertha Moritz and Gottfried Ritter between 1917 and 1918. Fred was born 7 Aug 1895, and died 20 June 1975[109] Rosella and Fred had two children.

22 vi. FANNY VOGELBACH was born in 1899 in Middletown, NY[110] and died on 10 Oct 1986 in Winthrop University Hospital, Mineola, NY.[111] She married JOSEPH WYLIE about 1921 in NY. Joseph was born 3 Dec 1898 in Gorestown, District of Benburb, Union of Dungannon, County Tyrone, Ireland and died on 7 Feb 1973 in Clearwater, FL.[112] Fanny and Joe Wylie are buried in Westbury Friends Cemetery, NY.[113] Fanny and Joe had three children.

23 vii. ADOLPH VOGELBACH was born in 1903,[114] probably in Jamaica, NY[115] and died 21 May 1984 in Charleston, WV. Adolph married DORIS HEIDTMANN on 14 Nov 1931 in Mineola, NY. Doris was born 9 Jun 1910 and died 28 July 2006 in Charleston, WV.[116] Adolph and Doris had one child.

24 viii. MARTHA VOGELBACH was born 28 Mar 1907 in Jamaica, NY[117] and died 14 Aug 2001 in Athens, OH.[118] She married WALLACE HEIDTMANN on 30 May 1935 in Hempstead, NY.[119] Wallace was born on 13 Feb 1907 in Sayville, NY and died on 31 Mar 1998 in Athens, OH.[120] Martha and Wallace are buried in Westbury Friends Cemetery. They had two sons.

---

[108] gravelocator.cem.va.gov, cites this information: Ritter, Fredrick John, Cox US Navy, World War I, Date of Birth: 08/07/1895, Date of death: 06/20/1975. Ritter, Rosella, wife of Ritter, Fredrick John, Date of Birth: 8/29/1897. Date of Death: 2/16/1982. Both are buried at: Section 2S Site 462, Long Island National Cemetery, 2040 Wellwood Avenue Farmingdale, NY 11735-1211.

[109] Certificate of Birth for Fredrick John Ritter, in the collection of Ruth Ritter, birth - Aug 7, 1895; Mother is Bertha Ritter from Switzerland; Father is Gottfried Ritter 36 yrs old from Baden; address is 1131 Tiffany Ave. near 167th St., Morrisania, Bronx.

[110] John Vogelbach Household, 1900 census, *op.cit,* daughter named "Fanny" was born July 1899. Eileen Greenlees said Jul 19 was her mother's birthday; she believed her mother was born in Middletown, NY.

[111] Death Certificate for Fanny Wylie, NYS Health Dept, District 2909, Register Number 741, 19 Jul 1999.

[112] Social Security Death Index at Ancestry.com.

[113] Westbury Friends Cemetery Records.

[114] Social Security Death Index on Ancestry.com for Adolph's birth and death dates.

[115] Certificate of Baptism for Joseph Vogelbach 27 March 1904 situates the family in Jamaica, NY.

[116] Social Security Death Index on Ancestry.com, cites Doris' birth and death dates.

[117] Certificate and Record of Birth for Martha Vogelbach on 28 March 1907 at 508 South Street, Jamaica, NY.

[118] Social Security Death Index at Ancestry.com for Martha's birth and death dates.

[119] Note from Peter Heidtmann to author in 2000 detailing births, marriages, and deaths in his family.

[120] Social Security Death Index at Ancestry.com for Wallace's birth and death dates.

Chapter 4

Florence Beyers and Joseph Vogelbach in Brooklyn or Queens, NY *circa* 1915. Photo is in the collection of the author.

Joseph VOGELBACH 1889 to 1952
Florence BEYERS 1887 to 1960

Joseph married a woman who was older than he, which always seemed curious to us as children.[1] We thought it was unusual for the husband to be younger than the wife, probably because in our experience the fathers of our cousins and friends were all older than the mothers. Since love was involved, age differences did not seem to bother Joseph and his wife Florence. There is a family story that Joseph's younger brother Louis was actually

---

[1] It is generally accepted that Florence was born on 19 November 1887. Joseph was born in 23 August 1889. We cannot corroborate the exact dates since neither of them had birth certificates. This was fairly typical for the 1800s. The month and year of their births is consistent with 1900 census records, however. And Nov 19 and Aug 23 were the days their respective families always celebrated their birthdays.

Florence's first love, and Louis was three and a half years younger than Florence. Apparently, Grandma went for younger men!

Florence graduated from a prestigious secretarial school in downtown Brooklyn called Heffley-Brown and worked as a stenographer in the early 1910s. Florence made friends easily. She liked to dress well, and the photos we have of her in her 20's show a trim, lovely young woman.

She evidently liked all the Vogelbach siblings, and remained close to Joseph's family for her whole life. We do not have a family story about how Florence and Joseph met, but they may have been introduced by Florence's Zahn cousins, who lived in Jamaica, Queens, near the Vogelbach residence. Grandma Mary Beyers, in her old age, was living with her daughter Amelia Zahn and her family. All the Beyers used to visit their grandma frequently when they could walk to her house in Brooklyn, and they probably took the long trolley ride to Jamaica to see her as often as possible after she moved there.

The trolley ride to Jamaica, with all the connections between Brooklyn and Queens, was more than two hours long. When the Long Island Electric Railroad (LIER) was finished, the trip to Queens was shortened considerably. The Beyers could then take a trolley to Flatbush Ave, get a ticket aboard the LIER, and get off three stops later at Sutphin Blvd. From Sutphin, it was an easy walk to the Zahn's house.

We can be pretty sure that Florence and her family were in Jamaica at least for Grandma Beyers' funeral service and burial in 1911 and probably on many other occasions. Florence could have met Louis and Joseph Vogelbach at church functions in Jamaica. The Zahns and Vogelbachs probably attended the same Lutheran church, St. Paul's, in Jamaica. Maybe the Vogelbach children and the Beyers and Zahn children all socialized together in the neighborhood during family visits to Queens. Florence was in her late teens and early twenties during this period.

Who knows when the spark between Florence and the Vogelbach boys was lit. Did Louis make the first move and then Joseph cut in? Louis was a very handsome, charming, and strong 20-year-old who worked summers on farms upstate, but he had no steady job. Did that discourage Florence? Or perhaps Louis' eyes may already have been on Rose Covington, which left an opening for Joseph to step in.

Joseph was also a strong and handsome young man, dashing in his Army Corps of Engineers uniform,[2] and he fell in love with Florence. They got to know each other better through

---

[2] Certificate of Death for Joseph Vogelbach, #64889, NY State, District 5154 Suffolk County: Joseph served in the US Armed Forces from 31 March 1908 to 18 March 1911. He was appointed Corporal on 1 Sept 1910 at Ft. DeRussy, Honolulu, Hawaii, according to his Appointment Certificate, in the collection of Veronica Black.

exchanging letters while Joseph was in Ft DeRussy, Hawaii, and while he was in Ohio helping to rebuild bridges as a civilian after the Great Ohio Flood of 1913.

Joseph always enjoyed working with his hands and wanted to find a construction job when he left his Corps service. In 1914, Joseph and Florence started talking about getting married, and his mother said, "You better get a steady job if you want to support a family." She actually got him the application for the NYC Police Department. This was a big mistake in Grace Vogelbach's opinion. She said, "My father was not cut out to be a policeman and didn't like his line of work. He really was a woodworking artist and loved to work with his hands." She believed the stress of being a policeman was the cause of his ill health, his strokes, and eventually his death. "Daddy was happiest when he was carving a piece of wood, whittling us toys, drawing, making some furniture, or building and repairing his house in Holbrook."

In any case, Joseph went through police training and was appointed Patrolman of the Police Force of the City of New York in 1914.[3] (Photo in the collection of the author.) Since he was now taking home a regular salary, Joseph and Florence could start planning their wedding.

A Mixed Marriage

It was customary to get married in the bride's church, so the couple spoke to a priest at Our Lady of Angels, Florence's home parish.[4] He told them that there were Roman Catholic Church rules governing "mixed marriages," rules intended to discourage Catholics from marrying Protestants. Florence had been raised Episcopalian but had converted to Roman Catholicism a few years before this. Now when she wanted to marry a Protestant, the church objected. How ironic! Joseph certainly did not intend to become a Catholic. His own father had rejected the Catholic religion. Family lore says that John and his brother Adolph left Switzerland partly to get away from their strict Catholic upbringing.

Joseph and Florence learned that they could not actually be married "in church." The ceremony would have to be in the rectory—the parlor of the priests' residence—and attended only by their witnesses, with no other family members or friends. Joseph also would have to swear and sign a statement that he would raise their children as Catholics, not as Lutherans or

---

[3] Police Department of the City of New York Appointment Certificate, 28 Feb 1914, in the collection of Veronica Vogelbach.
[4] Florence's home parish was Our Lady of Angels because she was living with her mother at 548 72nd Street, between 5th and 6th Avenues.

any other Protestant denomination.[5] All this probably caused a great deal of anguish for the young couple and their families as the wedding day approached, considering how emotional people become about religion and family tradition. Nevertheless, Joseph agreed to everything out of love for Florence, and they were married on 12 Oct 1915 in Our Lady of Angels rectory. The young assistant pastor, Rev. Charles Reilly, officiated. Their two witnesses were Joseph's sister Olga and Olga's fiancé Julius Jargstorff.[6]

This glass sugar and creamer set was a wedding gift from Florence's very close friend whom we all called Aunt Sadie. The set is in the collection of the author, who proudly uses the set whenever family comes to dinner.

Religion

Joseph Vogelbach kept his word about raising his children Catholic, and Grace said her dad was very strict about making them all attend Mass every Sunday. He did not go to church with them, though, and never became a Catholic. Grace said she used to go to two Sunday services. First, she would go to Our Lady of Angels with her mother and her sisters, and then she would run down to 80st Street to attend the Episcopal services at St. Phillip's so she could be with her Helliesen cousins, who were all so much fun.

Bay Ridge Residences

After they were married, Florence and Joseph lived for a couple of years with Florence's mother Susannah Beyers on 72nd Street, probably to help Susannah out. Florence's oldest girls Virginia and Grace were born there.[7] Grace's birth was during the flu pandemic of 1918, during World War I. This particular flu was a major factor in the deaths of millions of soldiers and civilians around the world.

Grace was told the following story of her birth, and she passed it down to us. "Hospital rooms were scarce, so my mother did not go to the hospital to give birth. Instead, family members tried to summon a doctor, and two doctors showed up by mistake. While they argued about who would go upstairs to attend the birth, I was born with Grandma Susannah Beyers assisting. Apparently, my birth was never recorded by the doctors or anybody else at

---

[5] The laws governing "mixed marriages" between Catholics and other baptized Christians were very strict until the 1970's.

[6] Church of Our Lady of Angels, 7320 Fourth Ave., Brooklyn, Marriage Register, 12 Oct 1915.

[7] The address actually was 548 72nd Street, between 5th and 6th Avenues, Bay Ridge, Brooklyn.

the Health Department. When I was in my 50's I wanted to visit Switzerland, and I found I needed a birth certificate to get a passport. My sister Virginia had to write the State Department a letter swearing that I was her sister and that I had been born in Brooklyn on Oct 19, 1918."

In 1919, Joseph's family moved to 7317 5th Ave. above Hyman's Butcher shop. Susannah Beyers and her son Charles and his second wife Catherine lived on the second floor, and the Vogelbach family lived on the third floor. Next door to Hyman's was Savastano's Grocery. Grace said that her mother often sent her downstairs to the butcher store or to Savastano's for something, and she just said, "Please put it on the books." The merchant wrote down the name Joe Vogelbach and noted whatever was bought that day. When Joseph received his paycheck at the end of the month, he settled the tab at both stores.

Ruth Ritter, one of our cousins, has a fond memory of the relationship between her Uncle Joe and Aunt Florence. She painted a sweet word picture of them: "Aunt Florence was petite, and Uncle Joe would pick her up and run up the stairs with her to their apartment in Brooklyn."

Joseph and Florence Raise a Family of Girls

Florence had six pregnancies. The first, which would have been a son, ended in a miscarriage. She then had five daughters: Virginia, Grace, Irene, Jean, and Joan. Irene died as a child. Photos below are in the collection of the author.

8 Aug 1921 Grace and Virginia

ca1930 Joan, Grace, Jean

Irene Vogelbach

Irene's Illness and Death

Grace remembered her sister Irene as a happy, impish child who had a tendency to throw tantrums when she couldn't get what she wanted. Sadly, Irene died when she was only three years old. Grace relates that, "Irene had pushed her high chair next to a built-in china cabinet to reach her new patent leather shoes which were on an open shelf. She slipped and fell, and cut her head. Mom cared for the wound, and it formed a scab. Irene picked at it, though. One day she was in her folding high chair, eating lunch, and was being very fussy. She banged her head against a brass knob on one of the lower kitchen cabinets, and the wound on her head became infected with erysipelas.[8] Mom got an erysipelas infection as well, but on her hand, and her infection healed. Every day a doctor came to clean Irene's wound, and to put new dressings on it. It just would not heal. One day, the doctor said he could not do anything more for Irene, and he admitted her into the hospital. My little sister Irene died the next day. Mom just kept rocking back and forth with her arms crossed over her chest and sobbing, 'My baby. My baby.' Her hair turned white overnight after Irene died; Mom was 37. Virginia and I stayed with relatives for several months."

Little Jean's Illness

Joan was born in 1925, the year after Irene's death. The family hardly had time to enjoy the new baby when Jean became very ill. Jean contracted diphtheria. Again, Virginia and Grace were sent to live with relatives. Aunt Anna and Uncle Joe Beyers and their daughter Mildred, who was about 18, took care of them. For the protection of baby Joan, and probably to give Florence a little break, Jean recuperated out on Long Island with friends of the family, a Mr. and Mrs. Buehn from Westbury.[9] The couple had no children, and the story is that they fell madly in love with Jean, who was bringing great joy into their home. They even wanted to adopt Jean, but, of course, Florence and Joseph said, "No!" Ruth Ritter remembers playing with Jean out in Long Island. The two of them stayed overnight with Mrs. Buehn when Grandma Fanny died. John Vogelbach was using the parlor in his Taylor Ave home for visitation and probably thought it best to get the grandchildren out of the house. That was 1927.[10] About the Buehns, "They had a big parrot," Ruth said, "and their home was near a famous restaurant near Old County Road and Post Ave. Mr. Buehn was a cook there. I also remember that Mrs. Buehn had gorgeous dahlias in her garden."

---

[8] *The Johns Hopkins Family Health Book* says that erysipelas is a bacterial skin infection, and it can spread rapidly. The skin takes on a vivid red color. The infected area is hot and painful and slightly elevated. It may be accompanied by fever, chills and vomiting. The disease was once known as "St. Anthony's Fire."

[9] Ernest Buehm Household, 1930 Census, NY, Nassau County, Hempstead, Westbury, ED 93, sheet 23A: Ernest and Marie Buehn lived on Old Country Road, around the block from the Vogelbach's Taylor Ave home. He was a chef at the Westbury County Club restaurant nearby.

[10] Kings Park State Hospital Register of Deaths, kept in Pilgrim Psychiatric Center, West Brentwood, NY: Fanny Vogelbach died at Kings Park on 24 Sep 1927. Undertaker was Turnure Undertaking Co., Hicksville, but Fanny was laid out at home. Jodi of Wagner Funeral, Hicksville told the author that they have a barometer labeled "Turnure Undertaking Co." on their wall. Perhaps Wagner's bought the Turnure business.

Life at home in Brooklyn took on a better rhythm when this period of illness and sadness passed. Joseph worked his shifts at the police department, and Florence did the usual cooking, cleaning, and making sure her girls did their homework. When Joseph worked the night shift, he slept during the day. The children had to be very quiet, which was hard for the four Vogelbach girls who had talkative personalities.

To relax in his spare time, Joseph whittled things out of wood and made beautiful furniture. He made this secretary, decorated with intricate carvings. The photo was taken by Betty Doheny. The secretary is in her home now.

The 1930's were hard times for most people because it was the Great Depression. Joseph's job as a policeman provided his family with security, and they did not worry about food or shelter as many people did. On the other hand, the Vogelbach family of six was very frugal. Wasting things was unheard of. Reuse and recycle was a way of life. The children wore hand-me-down clothing from older siblings and cousins. Shoes were repaired when heels got run-down, and cardboard inserts covered up holes in the soles of shoes.

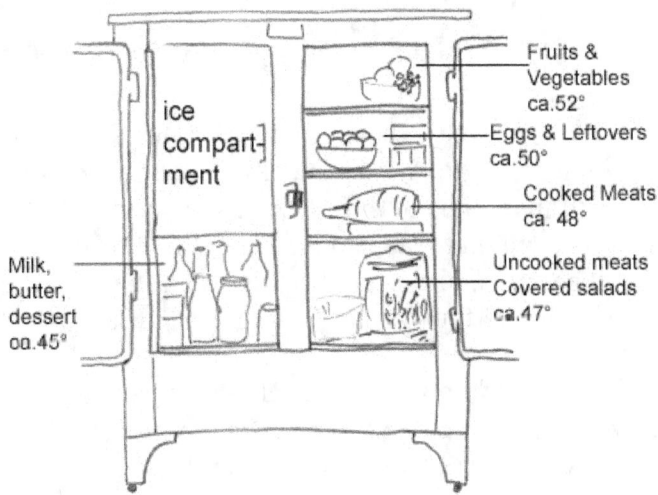

Florence had an ice box in the kitchen.[11] The "ice man" climbed the stairs once a week with a huge block of ice slung behind him on an ice pick. He put the ice in a special compartment - upper left in this drawing - to keep food cold for another week.

Gas lamp sconces provided light at night in their apartment, and their building was heated with coal from a furnace in the basement.

---

[11] Drawing is by the author, after a photo at http://en.wikipedia.org/wiki/Icebox.

Joseph and Florence's Home in Holbrook

Around 1930, Joseph bought an inexpensive piece of property out in Holbrook, about 50 miles east of Brooklyn. He built a bungalow with his own hands. The family went out every weekend to work on it. His daughter Grace boasted that she helped him with construction. Joseph bought a Ford at this time, too, to drive the family out to Long Island.

The earliest photo (at left) we have of the house has this note written on the reverse side: "Daddy & our bungalow, July 1931." The house continued to grow, first with the addition of a window under the front eaves, then a fireplace in the living room, a kitchen with a hand pump to draw potable water, and a back porch. A basement was dug, then an entire wing with two bedrooms, an attic, and an indoor bathroom was added. This August 1947 photo (at right) shows the finished house. Both photos are in the collection of the author.

Joseph retired from the NYC police force in 1940, and that same year his daughter Virginia married Edward Black. Now that their children were growing up and going out on their own, Joseph and Florence started spending more and more time in their "bungalow," and in 1942 they moved to Holbrook to live year round.[12] Grace and Jean had graduated high school, were working in New York, and living together in Flatbush near Virginia and Eddie. Joan was still in High School and would be the only one to finish school out on Long Island.

Florence had her favorite pastimes out on Long Island, too: bingo, church picnics, tending houseplants, and letter writing. Her activities were curtailed to some extent by high blood pressure and varicose veins compounded by a condition called phlebitis; her legs gave her a lot of trouble.

---

[12] Certificate of Death for Joseph Vogelbach, NYS Dept of Health, Suffolk Co, Reg# 570, stamped # 64889. The certificate says that Joseph was a full time resident of Holbrook for 10 years prior to his death in 1952.

Grandma had a habit of rolling her stockings below her knees; just one of those funny things you remember. In this photo, it looks like Joan and Jean are teasing her about her stockings. All the photos on this page are in the collection of the author.

Fishing was one of Joseph's summer pleasures. At right is a 1938 photo taken at Fire Island. Joseph is wearing the dark pants. The man on the right MAY be Eddie Black.

Joseph's Eldest Daughter Virginia

John Black said, "I think my mother very much relished her role as 'big sister' to everyone. A warm-hearted person by nature, she was very generous, and would go out of her way to help others. Virginia was very active in church affairs at St. Joseph's in Ronkonkoma, and one of my frustrations in life was to see, for instance, a cake on top of the refrigerator that we couldn't touch, because it was destined for one of the many bake sales used to raise money for church activities. An accomplished seamstress, she often made clothes for herself and Veronica. Later in life, she made doll clothing for several people. Curious about a variety of topics, she loved to talk. In fact, one inside family joke was that when she arose every morning around 6:30, she would take a deep breath, and continue talking until the sun went down."

Virginia's husband Edward Black had been brought up by a kind blind woman in Brooklyn named Mrs. Brennan, who took in "waifs."[13] As an adult, Edward worked as a UPS driver in Brooklyn. He commuted to that job after he moved to Holbrook. He weathered several long and severe teamster strikes during his 30-year career with UPS. He

---

[13] Michael Brennan Household, 1920 Census, NY, Kings ED 474, Sheet 1-A. Edward Black, eight years old, was enumerated as a boarder in the household of Michael and Mary Brennan on 67th Street, Brooklyn. Kenny James, a five year old, was also enumerated with the family. Michael Brennan was a shipyard machinist.

was a very a resourceful person, however, and found all sorts of odd jobs to earn money for his family during the strikes. After he retired from UPS, he took at job with the Town of Islip as a truck driver.

Eddie loved sports of all kinds and was very athletic himself. John Black says, "I can remember when he was in his 50's, still able to compete with high school kids in pick-up baseball games. Besides sports, he enjoyed fishing and gardening. He always whistled when he worked around the house." When Eddie collapsed at age 63, his daughter Veronica, a registered nurse, tried to give him CPR, but he had died almost instantly of a massive heart attack, and her frantic efforts could not revive him.

Veronica was Joseph and Florence's first grandchild, and she remained the only grandchild for four and a half years. Her earliest memory of Grandpa was of a tall, angular, wiry person who was much more lenient with her than he had been with his own children. Veronica remembers Grandpa taking her for ice cream in his old Ford. The two of them would barrel down Coates Ave, splashing through puddles, dirtying up the isinglass windows,[14] with Veronica blowing the "ay-ooo-gah" horn.

Virginia was plagued by heart trouble, but she still traveled all over the country to visit her children and grandchildren. Virginia died in 1999.

The Second Daughter, Grace

Photo of Grace Vogelbach, *circa* 1923, in the collection of the author.

Grace described herself as a "tomboy." She said she loved playing stickball with the boys, running around the park, climbing trees, and getting her hands dirty.

She enjoyed being the athletic sister, and she did not think of herself as an especially "good student." As a senior in Girls Commercial High School, she worked very hard for good grades and qualified for membership in the athletes' honor society called Taeda. She was very proud of achieving that honor,

---

[14] Isinglass was not actually glass. It was a transparent substance, something like clear vinyl, used for the windows of some early automobiles. Isinglass was often made of mica, but the windows could be rolled up and snapped to the window frames. http://www.seagrant.wisc.edu/greatlakesfish/lakesturgeon.html explains that, *"A gelatin from the inner lining of the [Great Lakes sturgeon] air bladder was used to make isinglass—the gelatin was a substance used as a clarifying agent in jellies, glues and in the isinglass windows of carriages and early cars."* The process of making isinglass was not described on this website.

and she always treasured her Taeda pin. That memento is on display in a shadow box in her daughter Anne's home in Florida.

When Grace was job hunting after High School, subway rides cost a nickel. On one of her hunts, she made an unannounced visit to her father's cousin Robert Vogelbach at the Kaleck Water Company, 30 Rockefeller Plaza, New York City. Robert was in upper management there and was most gracious to her. He took her out to lunch, but didn't have a job for her. He did give her kind advice, though. "I suggest you wear stockings instead of anklets when you appear at a job interview. They will make you look more professional." Grace thanked him very much for the lunch and the good advice. Many years later, when Grace told this story to her children, she still marveled at how naïve she was as a nineteen-year-old.

Grace told us another story about her job hunting days in 1937. Her cousin Mildred Beyers arranged for her to have an interview at her husband's company.[15] Grace was an excellent typist, and likely would have gotten the position, but she was so nervous while she was filling out the application that she misspelled "typist," and, of course, that disqualified her.

At last, Grace was hired by Western Union in downtown Manhattan, first as a "route aide" for $0.31 an hour, working four hours a day, five days a week, then as a typist earning $0.33 an hour. She asked Virginia and Eddie Black if she could live with them for a while, and they agreed. After Veronica was born, Virginia needed a little more space in the apartment for the new baby, so Grace and her sister Jean, who was also working by then, rented a tiny apartment nearby. Grace and Jean commuted to the city together.

Photo at right, in the collection of the author, is of Grace working as an inter-office messenger in Western Union. Notice the roller skates she is wearing. Grace brought memos from one employee to another; there were no computers, faxes, or even the suction tubes you might see at banks today to transfer time-sensitive material from one employee to another.

While she worked at Western Union, Grace met Bernard Doheny who was a typist there. Bernard asked Grace for a date, and she suggested going to a roller rink. She asked Bernard if he knew how to skate, and

---

[15] Mildred's father-in-law Robert Ryan owned a publishing company.

he said shyly, "A little." When they got there, Bernard opened up a box holding a pair of his own roller skates. It turned out that he was an accomplished skater whose hobby was dancing on skates. They had a wonderful time on such dates and soon fell in love.

Bernard and Grace were married 21 Aug 1943[16] while Bernard was on a one week leave from active duty in the US Army. Florence and Joseph advised Grace against marrying a soldier, but the couple was in love, and Grace resisted her parents' pressure. Bernard was a MSGT (described as Sgt Major 502 on his Separation Record) and would serve in a head-quarters company in the war in Europe from Jan 22, 1944 to Oct 29, 1945.

At right are Florence and Joseph dressed for the wedding. Both photos are in the collection of the author.

After the war, Bernard worked for Goldman Sachs as an internal accountant, a position he would hold for 33 years. His first salary was $35 a week, which came to approximately $1,820 for all of 1946. His family depended on the Goldman Sachs end-of-year bonuses to its employees for a good portion of its needs. Bernie made about $15,000 a year in base pay when he retired in 1979. His bonuses sometimes amounted to another $4,000.

Grace's first daughter Catherine, the author, was born within the year after Bernie returned from World War II. The young family left their one-room rental apartment in Flatbush, Brooklyn ($10 a week), and moved to temporary housing in the Quonset huts in Canarsie which the federal government had set up for WW II veterans. Their second daughter, Anne, was born while they lived in Canarsie.

---

[16] Certificate of Marriage of Bernard and Grace Doheny, Our Lady of Refuge RC Church, Brooklyn, NY.

Heating for a Quonset hut came in the form of a kerosene space heater. Grace said she would put a large brown five-gallon can in the carriage with baby Anne, while Catherine hung on the handle of the carriage. She did her food shopping on Avenue L, which was quite a walk with a carriage, a baby, and a toddler. Sometimes she would leave her little children with Bernie, and she would go to the stores a second time by bus to bring home a few more bags of groceries. They had to spend some extra money on certified milk for Catherine, and Anne would only keep her milk down if Grace mixed some Karo Syrup in it. Another added expense was Buster Brown shoes for Catherine's very narrow feet. But the family saved money in other ways because they used hand-me-down clothes from relatives and friends. Sharing clothes and using second-hand furniture was pretty common among struggling families in the late 1940's and the 1950's after World War II. Right after the war, manufactured goods were not readily available. Grace got on a waiting list at Abraham & Straus department store to buy a sewing machine. The Doheny family did not have a telephone before moving to Long Island in 1954, so Grace had to go down to a public phone booth to keep calling A&S about her machine, which she eventually bought for about $70 (about $500 in today's currency). She became an accomplished dressmaker and even made spring coats and Sunday dresses for her children.

In 1949, the Doheny family moved to the Gowanis Apartments, a public housing project in downtown Brooklyn. They lived on the eighth floor of a fourteen-story building. Another daughter, Elizabeth, was born while the family lived there. Finally, in 1954, the Doheny family moved to its very own home in Plainview which was bought with a 30-year VA mortgage for $9,999. Grace's fourth daughter Margaret was born in Plainview, and Bernie said they were not going to move any more. He said every time they moved, Grace got pregnant! Bernie commuted everyday to downtown Manhattan. His long daily rides to and from the city, though, ensured a wonderful place on Long Island to raise his children.

Photo at right was taken on the occasion of Grace and Bernard's fifth wedding anniversary, 1948, in Canarsie. The photo is in the collection of the author.

Grace and her sisters took their families for frequent trips out to Holbrook to see Joseph and Florence. For the grandchildren, life in Holbrook was a novel change from their city and suburban experiences. Grandpa raised chickens behind his house in Holbrook, and the grandchildren were expected to feed the animals and collect the eggs. In this 1952 photo, Anne and Catherine Doheny are doing some chores. Later, Grandma would pass a candle behind each egg to look for a spot of blood near the yolk. Blood indicated an egg was fertilized, and she said it would not taste good. (I still remember the thrill of eating fresh eggs for breakfast from Grandpa's own chickens.)

The children were often entertained watching Grandpa roll his own cigarettes. He shook a little tobacco out of a pouch into precut paper, rolled it up, and licked the edge to make it hold together. Grandpa also smoked a pipe, a fragrance that even today can conjure his presence. John Black's early memories of Grandpa painted him as "a 'Renaissance man' of sorts. He not only built his own house, carved figurines, and made furniture, but also played the mandolin, dabbled in horticulture, and drew murals on the plasterboard in the chicken coop in the back yard." John said, "One vivid memory I have of him was this: as he was propped up in bed, he would light a wooden kitchen match with his thumbnail and ask me to blow out the flame. Once the smoke cleared, he would use the resulting charcoal at the end of the match to draw something on a piece of paper or cardboard."

Joseph's Strokes

In early 1952, after Joseph suffered a stroke, Virginia, Grace, and Joan and their children took turns staying for a week at a time with their parents to help them out. The Doheny family, for example, would take the Long Island Railroad to Holbrook and walk a mile from the station to Grandma and Grandpa's house. Grandma would greet us with big noisy kisses on our cheeks that tickled. She smelled pleasantly of talc and ivory soap, and enveloped us in enormous hugs when we arrived.

After his stroke, Joseph walked with a shuffle and needed a cane. He had carved his cane himself, with a rhino head on the handle. He was not always dressed, and he shaved less often; his beard was stubbly and rough. He still liked to be around the grandchildren, though.

When Grandpa finally became bed-ridden, his grandchildren would run around his bed and play hide and seek with him. Even lying in bed, his reflexes were phenomenal; his grip was like a vice. He laughed at the game, but could also hurt your arm without meaning to. The next day, we would do it all over again.

Here is a 1952 photo, in the collection of the author, of Grandpa and Grandma surrounded by Joe and Mike Martin, Catherine, Anne, and Betty Doheny, and Veronica Black.

Joseph Died in 1952

Grandpa suffered another stroke at Wildwood State Park[17] in the summer of 1952 during a family picnic. Bernie Doheny and Eddie Black tried to keep him comfortable on one of the picnic benches while the other family members anxiously awaited the ambulance. Everyone was so upset, and the rest of the day was a blur. Joseph died a few months later at age 63 of yet another stroke. On his death certificate, the cause of death was "Uremia (meaning a coma), arteriolar nephrosclerosis and arteriosclerosis." There was also a notation that he had suffered from hypertensive heart disease for more than the last four years of his life.[18] Joseph was buried in an Episcopal cemetery in Sayville, since he was a Protestant.[19] Children were not allowed to go to the wake at the funeral parlor, except Veronica, the oldest grandchild.

Virginia's family moved out to Holbrook soon after Grandpa died. Her children all attended St. Joseph's Elementary School in Ronkonkoma, which was a long school bus ride from their home.

The House in Holbrook Holds So Many Memories

At Thanksgiving and Christmas, and many weekends during the summer months, the whole extended family gathered in Holbrook. John Black says, "Sometimes there would be impromptu competitions of baseball, rope-jumping, and other games of skill. But one contest that always comes to mind was a whistling competition between your mother and my father. Both of them could produce ear-splitting sounds by sticking their fingers in their bottom lips as they blew. In order to determine who was loudest, they went down to the main road

---

[17] Joseph's granddaughter Anne can see this park from her home in Baiting Hollow.

[18] Certificate of Death for Joseph Vogelbach, *op.cit,* Joseph died at home in Holbrook at 7 pm on 23 Oct 1952.

[19] Memorial Card for Joseph Vogelbach, "Services for Joseph A. Vogelbach, born August 23, 1889, Flushing, NY, Died October 23, 1952, Holbrook, NY, held at Raynor's Memorial Chapel, Sayville, NY, Sunday, October 26, 1952; 2P.M., Clergyman, Rev. Louis H. Martin. Interment at St. Ann's Cemetery, Sayville, NY." St. Ann's is an Episcopal Cemetery, Catherine Helliesen Andersen told me.

(Coates Avenue), and paced off a distance of a block or two, then kept on increasing the distance, until it was about a half-mile. My father would never admit it, but I think I remember your mother coming up on top."

Every summer, Grace and Virginia "swapped" children. Elizabeth Doheny listed her fond memories of that time:

"Marita came to our house when Anne went to Aunt Virginia's. Actually, Marita and I continued staying at each other's houses long after the older cousin swap fest ended. I would stay in Holbrook for a week or two and Marita would stay with us the following week or two. I remember going for a very long walk with Uncle Eddie and Marita one hot afternoon. I was more thirsty that day than I have ever been in my life. I also remember being fascinated by the orange day lilies that grew along side the road on Coats Ave.

"Uncle Eddie always liked to buy us butter pecan ice cream. It was a forbidden fruit for him because of his diabetes, but he loved it and thought it would be a great treat for us, too. He couldn't understand why, if it wasn't chocolate, it wasn't a treat for me.

"Marita and I ate about 10 pieces of toast everyday for breakfast one year. We both put on a few pounds but I'm sure that is why we are taller than all the other female cousins.

"I inhaled my first cigarette. Some local girl pointed out to everyone how I made it look like I was smoking but I wasn't even inhaling. Wanting to prove her wrong, I took a drag and choked. I hated the feeling in my lungs. I didn't like her too much either. Fortunately, it ended my attraction to tobacco.

"Marita and I really didn't want to go on a girl scout outing to an old age home in "Yang-a-Pang" (Yapank), but Aunt Virginia must have been a driver or somehow involved because she insisted that we go.

"Marita and I tried everything. The funniest thing was trying to get Marita to throw up by putting her finger down her throat. She just kept laughing.

"One year I brought a hair straightener kit with me. I hated my curly hair. I didn't think Aunt Virginia would notice, and I knew my mother would object. Marita helped me do it, and it stunk to high heaven. We might have been down in the basement because I remember Aunt Virginia yelling from outside, "What are you kids up to now? What is that horrible smell?" We said, "Nothing," and laughed and laughed. For a few wonderful hours that one afternoon in my life, I had the magnificent feeling of smooth silky hair easily falling between my fingers. That evening the weather turned foggy and the kink was back.

"Remember going blueberry picking? I remember going with many cousins, although it might have been just us and the Blacks, so it must have been one of those Sunday dinners in Holbrook. I didn't like blueberries, but I thought it was so cool to go into the woods and collect food. We were all given paper cups and told not to come back until they were full. I think the adults just didn't want us around the house."

Virginia was more lenient than Grace was, at least that is the way it seemed to the Doheny girls. We rode bicycles for miles, went swimming in Lake Ronkonkoma, ran through the woods behind the house, read comic books, listened to popular music, camped overnight in the old chicken coop, and explored Grandpa's old stuff in the basement.

Photo, summer of 1953,
in the collection of the author.
Betty Doheny, Michael Martin, Gregory Black,
Anne Doheny, Joe Martin, Catherine Doheny,
and Johnny Black are playing under the
sprinkler in the back yard in Holbrook.

Grace saved one of her daughter Anne's letters from Holbrook written during one of the cousins' exchanges. Anne was not quite nine years old when she wrote this. It is included here with Anne's permission.

July 12, 1956

Dear Mother,
I am writing this letter to ask you and daddy welher I could keep Bushtail. (Bustail is a scuril) Bushtail was ingered and can't move his left arm. I hope you and the girls are fine. I'll have to say to Catherine I miss her because she will get mad at me. I realy don't because I ride Greggy's bike every day and I have Bushtail. Greggy just woke up now. By the way Bushtail can't see. I got a new toothbrush. It is green and made of nyolan.
Love Anne

John Black says, "I was also part of the summer kid exchange program, going to the Doheny's house for a week. For me, it was a bit of independence, going to a nearby school for summer camp activities like basket-weaving and, of course, baseball. At night, I would talk with Uncle Bernie about baseball, while he sat calmly in his favorite chair drinking his glass of pilsner beer."

Florence Died in 1960

Grandma Florence died 15 May 1960 in Holbrook, NY[20] at age 71. It was on a Sunday, and was one of those rare days that Florence was not well enough to go to Mass. The family always ate their big meal in the middle of the day on Sundays. In the evening Florence and Virginia were sitting at the dining room table having tea, and the TV was on. Florence said, "Eddie, get your head out of the way. I can't see the TV." Then she put her cup down, and said, "I feel…," and collapsed.[21] Their doctor was called and he told the family that Florence died of a massive heart attack. He said she probably died instantly, with no pain, which was always a consolation to the family. She was buried in Holy Sepulcher Cemetery, Coram, NY,[22] a Catholic cemetery, and not with her husband Joseph.

Author's closing comments…

When I graduated from elementary school in June 1960, my mother gave me a present from Grandma, which she had bought for me right before she died. The gift was a gold chain with a delicate pearl and gold pendant on it. When I entered the convent of the Sisters of Mercy, my mother kept the necklace in her jewelry box. She gave it back to me when the sisters were permitted to wear lay clothing. Many Sisters then wore simple jewelry. After I left the convent, I continued wearing it and thought of my wonderful Grandma. The year after I got married, our home was burglarized, and Grandma's gift was among the precious items that the burglars stole. Things disappear or are stolen, but memories can last much longer. I hope this book preserves and celebrates many precious family memories for my readers.

Catherine

---

[20] Memorial Card for Florence E. Vogelbach, Florence died 15 May 1960 at age 71. Wake was at Joseph A. Weber Funeral Home, Lake Ronkonkoma, LI.

[21] Veronica Black related these events, as told to her by her mother, Virginia, who was present when Florence died.

[22] Florence was not buried with Joseph, since Joseph was buried in a Protestant cemetery. Catholic Church rules were very strict in the 1960's. Virginia and Eddie Black would one day be buried in Holy Sepulcher Cemetery, next to Florence.

Genealogical Summary

18. JOSEPH ANTHONY[2] VOGELBACH (*John[1], Anton[A]*) was born 23 Aug 1889 in Corona, Flushing, NY[23] and he died 23 Oct 1952 in Holbrook, NY.[24] Joseph married Florence Elizabeth Beyers on 12 Oct 1915 in Brooklyn.[25] Joseph was a NYC policeman.[26]

The children of Joseph Vogelbach and Florence Beyers are:

Grace, Virginia, Jean, and Joan, on Shore Road, Bay Ridge, Brooklyn, *circa* 1940. Photo is in the collection of the author. Florence always kept a copy of this photo on her bedroom dresser.

42. VIRGINIA[3] VOGELBACH (*Joseph[2], John[1], Anton[A]*) was born 5 May 1917 in Bay Ridge, Brooklyn, NY. She died on 5 April 1999 at Brookhaven Memorial Hospital. She married Edward Black on 17 Aug 1940 in Our Lady of Angels Church, Bay Ridge, Brooklyn. Edward was born 11 March 1911 in NY. He died on 23 October 1974 in their home in Holbrook, NY. They had two girls and two boys.

---

[23] Certificate of Baptism for Joseph Vogelbach, St. Paul's Lutheran Church, Jamaica. Joseph was born on 23 Aug 1889 in Corona, NY and baptized many years later on 27 May 1904 in Jamaica, NY.

[24] Certificate of Death for Joseph Vogelbach, NYS Dept of Health, District 5154, Registered # 570.

[25] Certificate of Marriage for Florence Beyer and Joseph Vogelbach in the Parish Register of Our Lady of Angels Roman Catholic Church, 7320 Fourth Ave., Brooklyn.

[26] Certificate of Appointment to the Police Department of the City of New York, 24 Feb 1914, in the collection of Veronica Black, Holbrook, NY.

43.   Grace Dolores Vogelbach was born 19 Oct 1918 in Brooklyn, NY, and died of "congestive heart failure – etiology unknown" on 5 November 2005 in South Venice, FL. [27] She married Bernard Greene Doheny 21 Aug 1943 in Brooklyn, NY, son of Edward Doheny and Katharine Greene. He was born 11 Oct 1913 in Brooklyn, NY, and died of sideroblastic anemia on 18 May 1989 in South Venice, FL. [28] They had four daughters. Grace and Bernie are buried in the VA Cemetery in Calverton, Long Island.

Grace was a full time homemaker until her oldest daughter (the author) entered the convent. Grace then worked as a cook for the Sisters of Mercy at St. Pius X School for four years. In 1968, when her youngest child started high school, Grace got a full time job as a secretary/office manager for Center Tool, Inc. at about $4,000 per year. Grace and Bernie used the money from that job to pay for yearly vacations, especially cruises. Photo below was taken at Bernard's 1979 retirement party, and is in the collection of the author.

Grace and Bernie moved to South Venice, Florida in 1979. The couple enjoyed ten happy years in Florida until Bernard's death in 1989 at age 75. Grace lived to be 87 years old. Almost to the end of her life, she bowled, played pinochle, and knitted sweaters for her grandchildren, flew frequently to New York to visit friends and family, and was an active member of her parish in South Venice. In her widowhood, she had a good friend and companion named Charles Spiroff. Charlie was her devoted friend until his death in December 2003.

After a long life with reasonably good health, Grace developed diabetes, high blood pressure, thyroid problems, and then suffered multiple minor strokes in the last five years of her life.

---

[27] Certificate of Death for Grace D. Doheny, Nov 5, 2005, State of Florida, Office of Vital Statistics.

[28] Certificate of Death for Bernard G. Doheny, May 18, 1989, State of Florida, Office of Vital Statistics.

44. IRENE VOGELBACH was born in Brooklyn on 15 Jan 1921. She died in 1924. Irene was buried with her Grandfather George Beyers in Green-Wood Cemetery.[29]

Irene Vogelbach, 1924, photo in the collection of the author.

45. JEAN FLORENCE VOGELBACH was born in Brooklyn on 2 March 1923 and died on 5 Jul 1992 in Kingston, New York.[30] She is buried in a small cemetery there. Jean married Francis Albert Buhse in 1948. Grace said they eloped. Frank Buhse was born 18 February 1921 in Brooklyn, NY and died 7 Jan 1980 in Brooklyn.[31] They had two daughters.

Frank suffered from ill health for many years. Jean, an office manager, was the primary wage earner in their family. After Frank died, Jean lived in Brooklyn for a while; then she moved upstate New York to the Kingston area to be closer to her grandchildren. Jean and Frank were known for their wit and humor. Photo was taken at Grace's house in the 1970's and is in the collection of the author.

Jean suffered from strokes near the end of her life, as did her father and her sister Grace.

---

[29] Green-Wood Cemetery online burial search at www.green-wood.com: Irene was buried on 8 April 1924. She's buried in Lot 31394, Section 128.
[30] Memorial Card for Jeanne Buhse, in the collection of the author.
[31] Social Security Death Index, Ancestry.com, and Memorial Card for Frank Buhse, in the collection of the author.

46. LIVING VOGELBACH married John Martin on 28 May 1948 in Holy Innocents Church, Brooklyn. Jack, as he was always called, was born 16 June 1924 in Brooklyn. He worked for the NY Daily News and injured his hand when a huge roll of newsprint rolled into him. He died 4 December 1993 in Brooklyn.[32] He is buried in Ashland, NY in the cemetery where many of his Martin relatives are buried. They had two boys and two girls.

---

[32] Memorial Card for John Martin, in the collection of the author: "In loving memory of John P. Martin, December 4, 1993"

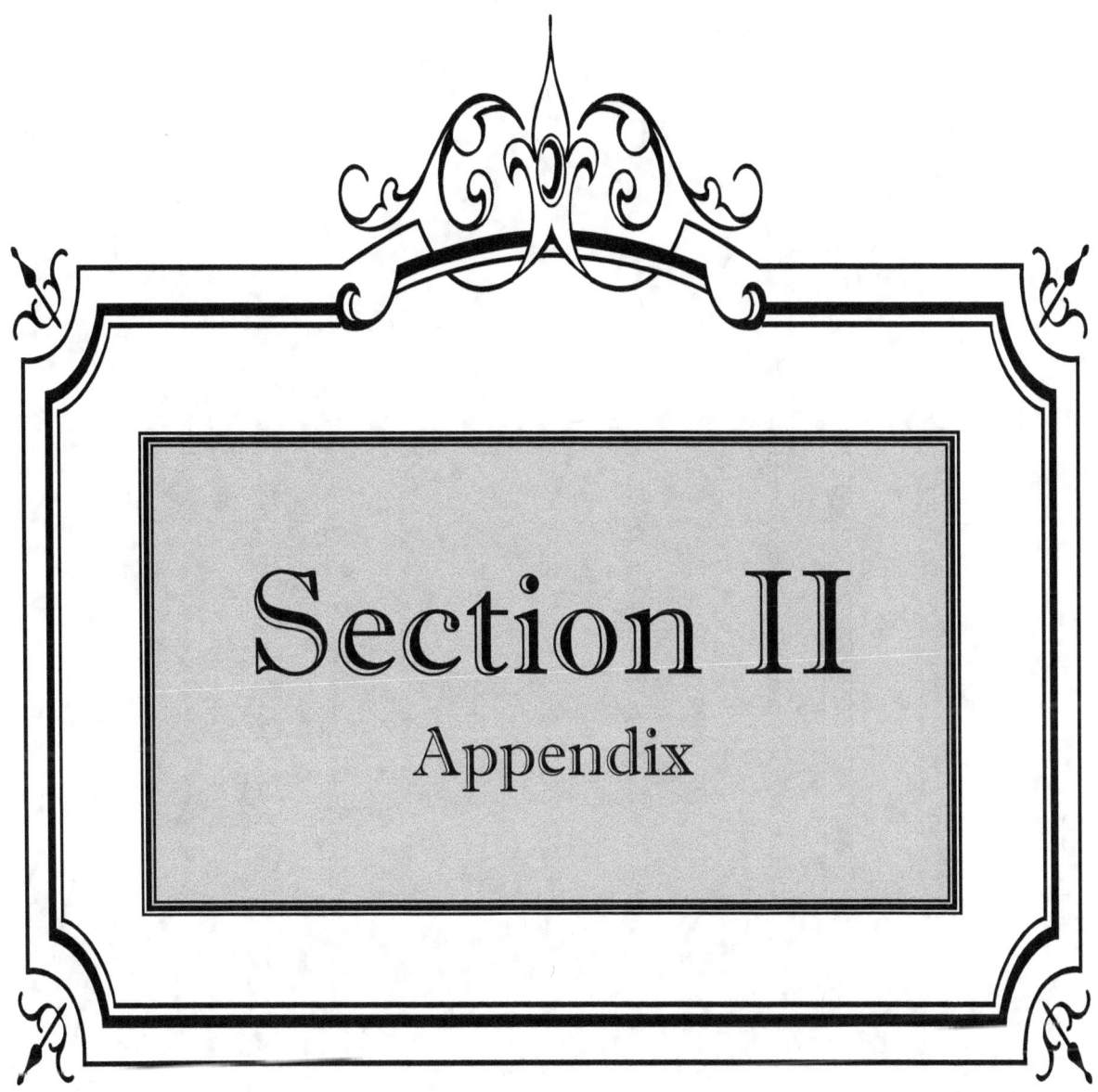

Section II
Appendix

A – Vogelbach Family Tree – Outline format

1 Anton VOGELBACH b: Bef. 1830 in Switzerland d: Unknown
.. +Elisabeth SCHNEEBELI b: Bef. 1830 in Affoltern am Albis, Switz. m: Bef. 1858 in Zürich, Switzerland d: Unknown
...... 2 Alexander VOGELBACH b: Bet. 1855 - 1870 in Switzerland d: Unknown
...... 2 Otto VOGELBACH b: Bet. 1855 - 1870 in Switzerland d: Unknown
...... 2 Robert VOGELBACH b: Bet. 1855 - 1870 in Switzerland d: Unknown
...... 2 Adolph VOGELBACH b: Jul 1858 in Switzerland d: 1926 in Town of Crawford, NY
.... +Barbara HASSLER b: Mar 1865 in Germany m: 23 Dec 1883 in Manhattan, NY d: 1959
.... 3 Adolph VOGELBACH b: Bet. 1885 - 1899 d: Bef. 1900
.... 3 Martha VOGELBACH b: Bet. 1885 - 1899 d: Bef. 1900
.... 3 Maximillian VOGELBACH b: Bet. 1885 - 1899 d: Bef. 1900
.... 3 Maximillian VOGELBACH b: Bet. 1885 - 1899 d: Bef. 1900
.... 3 Olga VOGELBACH b: Bet. 1885 - 1899 d: Bef. 1900
.... 3 Robert VOGELBACH b: 23 Jan 1888 in Brooklyn, New York d: Jan 1969 in St. Petersburg, FL
.... +Friederika WAECHTER b: 8 Jun 1887 in New York m: Abt. 1909 d: 4 Feb 1977 in Andover, Sussex, NJ
.... 4 Helen VOGELBACH b: 17 Nov 1913 d: Oct 1983 in Maywood, Bergen Co, NJ
.... +William ECKEL b: 1906 m: Abt. 1938 d: 1986
.... 3 Elfrieda VOGELBACH b: Feb 1891 in New York d: Bet. 1920 - 1930 in NJ or CT
.... +Fred ANDERSON b: 1888 in NJ m: Abt. 1911 in New Jersey d: Bef. 1980
.... 4 Frederick ANDERSON b: 1912 in NJ d: Unknown
.... 4 Edmund ANDERSON b: 1913 in NJ d: Unknown
.... 4 Living ANDERSON
.... 3 Oscar VOGELBACH b: 25 Jan 1897 in Montgomery, Orange Co, NY d: 27 Dec 1959 in Thompson Ridge, NY
.... +Eleanor Woods LINDSAY b: 26 Feb 1899 in Kearny, NJ m: 6 Mar 1918 in Kearny, NJ d: 2 Dec 1983 in NY
.... 4 Eleanor VOGELBACH b: 1919 d: 1925
.... 4 Ethel VOGELBACH b: 10 May 1922 in NJ d: 12 Jul 2006 in Goshen, NY
.... +Charles ROEBUCK b: 29 Oct 1921 m: 1946 d: 19 Jun 1988 in New York
.... 4 Robert VOGELBACH b: 11 Nov 1923 d: 26 Sep 1992 in Thompson Ridge, NY
.... +Jean THOMPSON b: 19 Feb 1925 m: 1951 d: 15 Oct 1997 in Thompson Ridge, NY
.... 4 Living VOGELBACH
.... +Walter ROEBUCK b: 12 Feb 1931 d: 20 Jan 1996 in Montgomery, Orange Co, NY
.... 4 Theodore Oscar VOGELBACH b: 18 May 1935 d: 10 Aug 2003 in Monroe, VA
.... +Living MARA
.... 3 Edmund Adolph VOGELBACH b: 21 Mar 1899 in Crawford, New York d: Bef. 1930 in Ridgefield, CT
.... +Phyllis BECK b: 25 Mar 1897 in NY m: Abt. 1924 d: Oct 1969 in Los Angeles, CA
.... 4 Living VOGELBACH
.... 3 Fanny VOGELBACH b: 15 Sep 1903 in NY d: May 1984 in Southbury, New Haven Co, CT
.... +Myron E. LEWIS b: 9 Jul 1900 in Southbury, CT m: Abt. 1924 d: 10 Dec 1990 in Waterbury, New Haven, CT
.... 4 Living LEWIS
.... +Living BAILEY
.... 4 Living LEWIS
.... +Alfred Harold JURGENS b: 1925 d: 2001
.... 4 Living LEWIS
.... +Leona BRYANT b: 1934 d: 1984
.... 4 Living LEWIS
.... 4 [1] Robert Edmund LEWIS b: 4 May 1930 in CT d: 12 Jun 1998 in Waterbury, CT
.... +Living ROWE
.... *2nd Wife of [1] Robert Edmund LEWIS:
.... +Living SMITH
.... 4 Living LEWIS
.... +Robert William CHAPMAN b: 14 Aug 1932 d: 8 Jun 2000
.... 4 Living LEWIS
.... +Living ELY

...... 2 John VOGELBACH b: 24 Apr 1862 in Küsnacht, Switzerland d: 8 Nov 1947 in Central Islip, NY
.... +Fanny Amalie MORITZ b: 5 Apr 1866 in Thalwil, Switzerland m: 21 Nov 1886 in NY d: 24 Sep 1927 in NY
.... 3 Otto Andreas VOGELBACH b: 9 Nov 1887 in Manhattan, NY d: 21 Nov 1952 in NY
.... +Lilly WASHING b: Abt. 1883 in Pennsylvania m: Bet. 1911 - 1916 d: Abt. 1946
.... 4 Son VOGELBACH b: Abt. 1917 in Washington DC d: Bef. 1920
.... 3 Joseph Anthony VOGELBACH b: 23 Aug 1889 in Corona, NY d: 23 Oct 1952 in Holbrook, NY
.... +Florence Elizabeth BEYERS b: 19 Nov 1887 in NY m: 12 Oct 1915 in NY d: 15 May 1960 in Holbrook, NY
.... 4 Virginia VOGELBACH b: 5 May 1917 in Brooklyn, NY d: 5 Apr 1999 in Holbrook, NY
.... +Edward BLACK b: 11 Mar 1911 in NY m: 17 Aug 1940 in Bklyn, NY d: 23 Oct 1974 in Holbrook, NY
.... 4 Grace Dolores VOGELBACH b: 19 Oct 1918 in Brooklyn, NY d: 5 Nov 2005 in So Venice, FL
.... +Bernard Greene DOHENY b: 11 Oct 1913 in NY m: 21 Aug 1943 in NY d: 18 May 1989 in FL
.... 4 Irene VOGELBACH b: 15 Jan 1921 d: 1924
.... 4 Jean Florence VOGELBACH b: 2 Mar 1923 in Brooklyn, NY d: 5 Jul 1992 in Kingston, NY
.... +Francis Albert BUHSE b: 18 Feb 1921 NY m: Abt. Feb 1948 in NY d: 7 Jan 1980 in Brooklyn, NY
.... 4 Living VOGELBACH
.... +John Patrick MARTIN b: 16 Jun 1924 in Brooklyn, NY d: 4 Dec 1993 in Brooklyn, NY
.... 3 Louis VOGELBACH b: 8 Apr 1891 in Flushing, NY d: 4 Aug 1973 in Chenango Bridge, NY
.... +Rose May COVINGTON b: Abt. 1873 in New York d: 20 Oct 1959 in Belfast, Maine
.... 3 Olga VOGELBACH b: 2 Dec 1894 in Crawford, NY d: 1 Aug 1984 in Brooklyn, NY
.... +Julius Ernst JARGSTORFF b: 20 Jan 1891 in Darmstadt, IL m: 16 Sep 1917 in NY d: 3 Nov 1977 in IN
.... 4 Living JARGSTORFF
.... +George Wendell HUGHES b: 18 Jul 1929 in Detroit, MI d: 10 Dec 1993 in Brookline, MA
.... 3 Rosella VOGELBACH b: 29 Aug 1897 in Crawford, Orange County, NY d: 16 Feb 1982 in Westbury, NY
.... +Frederick John RITTER b: 7 Aug 1895 in Bronx, NY m: Bet. 1917 - 1918 in NJ d: 20 Jun 1975 in NY
.... 4 Living RITTER
.... +Gertrude F. b: 19 Sep 1918 d: 9 May 1999 in Port St Lucie, FL
.... 4 Living RITTER
.... +Francis Xavier BUSH b: 22 Jul 1918 in Flushing, NY d: 5 May 1997 in Westbury, NY
.... 3 Fanny VOGELBACH b: 19 Jul 1899 in Middletown, NY d: 10 Oct 1986 in Mineola, NY
.... +Joseph WYLIE b: 3 Dec 1898 in Co Tyrone, North Ireland m: 1921 in Westbury, NY d: 7 Feb 1973 in FL
.... 4 Living WYLIE
.... +Living WISSLER
.... 4 Frances Eileen WYLIE b: 12 Feb 1926 in Westbury, NY d: 7 Sep 2004 in Williamsport, MD
.... +James GREENLEES b: 1925 in Westbury, NY m: 17 Jun 1950 in NY d: 15 Nov 2002 in MD
.... 4 Beverly WYLIE b: 3 Jan 1931 in Westbury, NY d: 29 Nov 2005 in Maryland
.... +Living HUTCHINSON
.... 3 Adolph VOGELBACH b: 21 Dec 1903 in Jamaica, NY? d: 21 May 1984 in Charleston, W V
.... +Doris E. HEIDTMANN b: 9 Jun 1910 in Hicksville, NY m: 14 Nov 1931 in Mineola, NY d: 2006 in W V
.... 4 Living VOGELBACH
.... +Living GATES
.... 3 Martha VOGELBACH b: 28 Mar 1907 in Jamaica, NY d: 14 Aug 2001 in Athens, OH
.... +Wallace HEIDTMANN b: 13 Feb 1907 in NY m: 30 May 1935 in Hempstead, NY d: 31 Mar 1998 in OH
.... 4 Living. HEIDTMANN
.... +Joan CROFT b: 31 Oct 1937 in NY d: 18 Jun 2002 in Athens, OH
.... *2nd Wife of Living HEIDTMANN:
.... +Living COLLINS
.... *3rd Wife of Living HEIDTMANN:
.... +Living STEWART
.... 4 Living HEIDTMANN
.... +Living STEVENS
...... 2 Mary VOGELBACH b: Aft. 1862 in Switzerland d: Unknown

Last names and relationships within the family have been included in this tree, but, to protect privacy, birthdates, marriage dates, and death dates have not been included.

B – Immigration Documentation for Our Ancestors

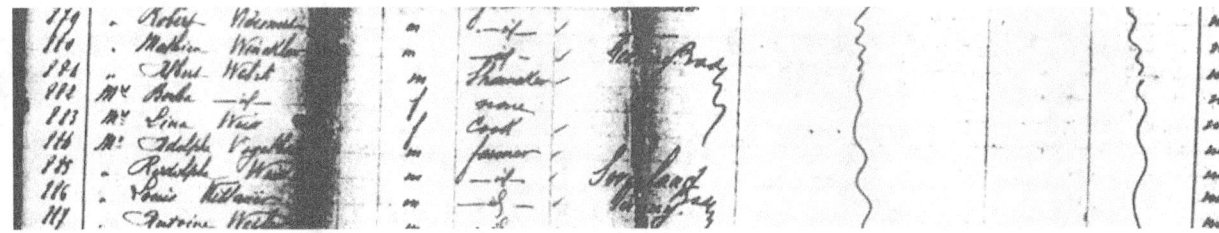

Line 884, Mr. Adolphe Vogelbach, male, farmer[1]

This MAY be our ancestor. The image is a detail of the passenger list of Schooner Levinia F Warren. Evidence against this being our Adolph is that there is no family story of Adolph having sailed from Europe via Macao, Brazil. On the other hand, Adolph's naturalization papers say he arrived in the US in May 1880.

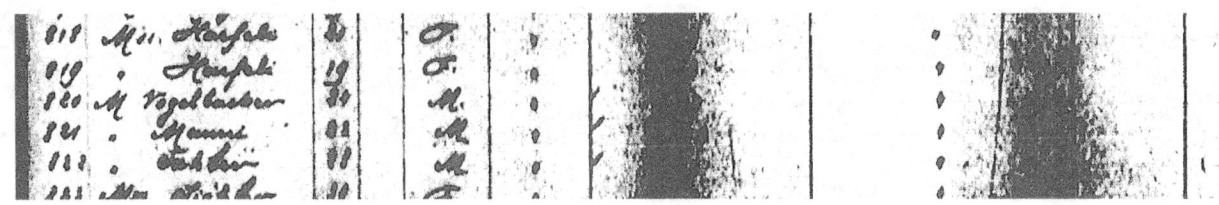

Line 820, Mr. Vogelbacker, 24, male, farmer, from Switzerland, bound for New York.[2]

This MAY be our John Vogelbach since 1882 is when several independent sources indicate that he arrived in America. Mr. Vogelbacker landed in New York from Le Havre aboard the S.S. France. Evidence against this being our John is that the age should be 20 in 1882.

Line 58, Fanny Moritz, 20, female, maid, Swiss, bound for New York, berthed in steerage, forward between deck, ladies only, one piece of baggage. This is DEFINITELY John's wife Fanny Moritz. Fanny's older sister Bertha, 25, maid, made the voyage with her. Bertha had two pieces of baggage. [3]

---

[1] Adolphe Vogelbach entry, *Schooner Levinia F Warren* Passenger List, 1 May 1880, page 10, line 884; New York Passenger lists 1820-1957, Ancestry.com. The Schooner left from Macao, Brazil. About half the passengers were Swiss.
[2] Mr. Vogelbacker entry, *S.S. France* Passenger List, 22 March 1882, line 820, New York Passenger Lists 1820-1957, Ancestry.com. The ship left from LeHavre, France
[3] Fanny Moritz entry, *S.S. France* Passenger List, 28 February 1884, page 2, line 58; New York Passenger Lists 1820-1957, Ancestry.com. The ship left from LeHavre, France.

C – Naturalization Documentation for Adolph Vogelbach

Family Name	Given Name or Names
	V 240
VOGEL	ADOLF

Title and Location of Court

COMMON PLEAS COURT. NEW YORK COUNTY.

Date of Naturalization	Volume or Bundle No.	Page No.	Copy of Record No.
OCT. 11-1888	657	–	76

Address of Naturalized Person

MORRIS AVE- N.Y.C.

Occupation	Birth Date or Age	Former Nationality
COPPERSMITH		SWISS

Port of Arrival in the United States	Date of Arrival
	MAY- 1880

Names, Addresses and Occupations of Witnesses To Naturalization

1 NILS LINDEBORZ- 433. E-14- ST.
2   N.Y.C.

[4] National Archives and Records Administration, Northeast Region, Soundex Index to Petitions for Naturalization filed in Federal, State, and Local Courts located in New York City, 1792-1989. New York, NY, USA: Copy found online at Ancestry.com. Reverse side of the card is blank.

D – *Marriage Record for Adolph Vogelbach and Barbara Hassler New York City, 23 December 1883*

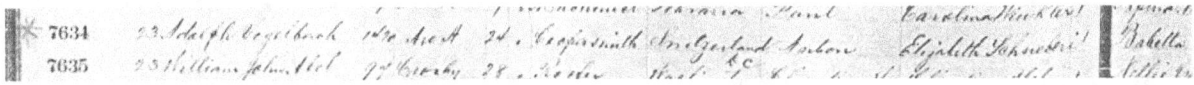

Adolph Vogelbach, residence 1420 Ave A, 24 years old, occupation coppersmith, born in Switzerland, father named Anton, mother named Elizabeth Schneberi

Babetta Haszler, residence 1420 Ave A, 20 years old, born in Germany, father named Johan G., mother named Ann M. Steller, wife's first marriage, presiding at the marriage was Adolph Berckmann, recorded Jan 2, 1884.

[5] Adolph Vogelbach and Barbara "Haszler" 23 Dec 1883 entry in NYC Registry of Marriages, Liber 7, Page 191, Line 7634, 1883. Copy acquired by the author from New York City Dept of Records and Information Services, Municipal Archives, 31 Chambers Street, New York, NY 10007

E – John Vogelbach's Application for Citizenship

United States of America.

STATE OF NEW YORK,
AND COUNTY OF NEW YORK, } ss.

Be it Remembered, That on the *14* day of *April*

... *one thousand eight hundred and eighty ...* personally

John Vogelbach

Superior Court of the City of New York (said Court being a Court of Record, having common

jurisdiction, a Clerk and a Seal), and made his declaration of intention to become a Citizen of

United States of America, in the words following, to wit:

John Vogelbach

... declare on oath, that it is *bona fide* my Intention to become a Citizen of the United States, and

... renounce forever all allegiance and fidelity to any foreign Prince, Potentate, State or Sovereignty

... ever, and particularly to the *Republic of Switzerland*

... whom I am a subject.

Sworn, this *14* day *April* 188*5*

John Vogelbach

Residence *421 ... St N. York*

THOMAS BOESE,
Clerk.

In Attestation Whereof, and that the foregoing is a true copy of the

original declaration of intention remaining of record ...

I, THOMAS BOESE, Clerk ... the said Superior Court, have hereunto

subscribed my name and affixed the seal of the Court, this

14 day of *April* 188*5*

Thomas Boese Clerk

---

[6] This document is in the collection of Veronica Black, Holbrook, NY.

F – John Vogelbach's Application for Citizenship – Transcription

United States of America

State of New York
City and County of New York

Be it remembered, that on the 14 day of April in the year of our Lord one thousand eight hundred and eighty five, personally appeared John Vogelbach in the Superior Court of the City of New York (said Court being a Court of Record, having common law jurisdiction, a Clerk and a Seal), and made his Intention to become a Citizen of the United States of America, in the words following, to wit:

I John Vogelbach do declare on oath, that it is bona fide my Intention to become a Citizen of the United States, and to renounce forever all allegiance and fidelity to any foreign Prince, Potentate, State or Sovereignty whatever, and particularly to the Republic of Switzerland of whom I am a subject.

Sworn, this 14 day of April 1885   John Vogelbach
Residence 421 East 76th Street, New York

Thomas Boese, Clerk

In Attestation Whereof, and that the foregoing is a true copy of the original declaration of intention remaining of record in my office, I Thomas Boese, Clerk of the said Superior Court, have hereunto subscribed my name and affixed the seal of the Court this

14th day of April 1885

Thomas Boese, Clerk

G – John Vogelbach's "Citizenship Papers"

---

[7] John Vogelbach's Naturalization Record, County Court, Queens County, NY, Family History Library Microfilm #1289052, Naturalization Records for 20 Oct 1892, Bundle 15, Record 209. Additional information in this record: "Address of Naturalized Person: 421 East 76th St., New York City."

H – John Vogelbach's "Citizenship Papers" – Transcription

Queens County Court
In the Matter of the Application of John Vogelbach for Admission to Citizenship
State of New York
County of Queens

W.H.Allen of said County, being duly sworn, each for himself doth depose and say that he is a citizen of the United States, that he is well acquainted with the above named John Vogelbach, that said John Vogelbach has resided within the limits and under the jurisdiction of the United States for five years last past, and for one year last past within the State of New York, and that during the same period he has behaved himself as a man of good moral character, attached to the principles of the Constitution of the United States and well disposed to the good order and happiness of the same,

Sworn in open Court the 20 day of Oct 1892 before me
J. H. Loughin, Clerk of Queens County

State of New York
County of Queens
John Vogelbach, the above named applicant, being duly sworn, doth depose and say, that for the continued term of five years last past, he has resided in the United States without being at any time within the said five years out of the territory of the United States, and that for one year last past he has resided within the State of New York.

I, John Vogelbach, applicant above named, do solemnly swear that I will support the Constitution of the United States; and that I do hereby absolutely and entirely renounce all allegiance and fidelity to all and every foreign Prince, Potentate, State and Sovereignty whatever, and particularly to Republic of Switzerland.

Sworn in open Court, before me, the 20 day of Oct 1892
J. H. Loughin, Clerk of Queens County.

On reading and filing the foregoing affidavit and declaration, it is ordered, that the above named applicant, John Vogelbach, be admitted, and is hereby accordingly admitted and declared to be a citizen of the United States of America. L.I.City Oct 20 – 92

J. H. Loughin
C. of Q. Co.

I – Marriage Certificate for John Vogelbach and Fanny Moritz

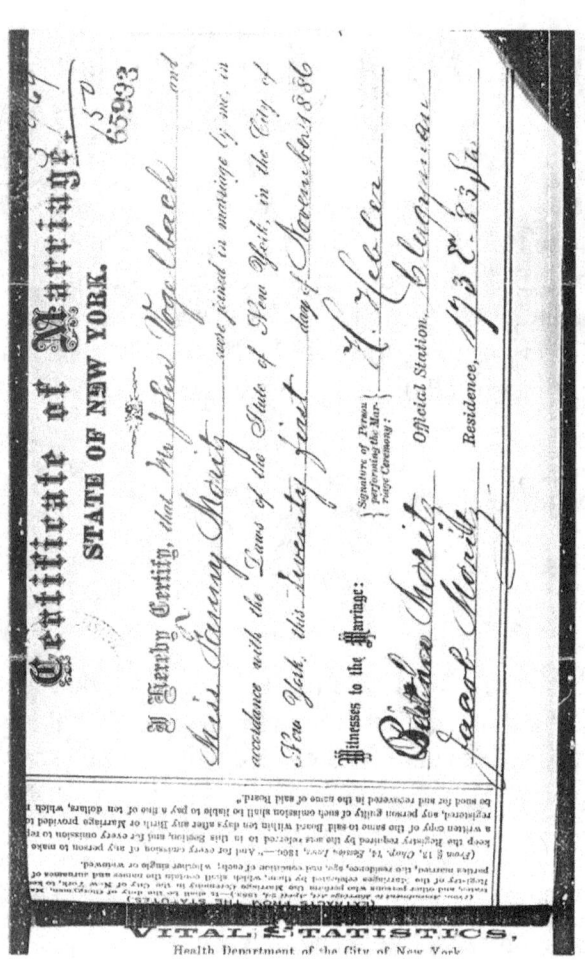

---

8 Certificate of Marriage for Fanny Moritz and John Vogelbach, 21 Nov 1886, Certificate# 65993, NYC Dept of Health, Municipal Archives, 31 Chambers Street, New York, NY 10007.

J – Marriage Certificate for John Vogelbach – Transcription

Certificate of Marriage - State of New York

I Hereby Certify, that Mr. John Vogelbach and Miss Fanny Moritz were joined in marriage by me, in accordance with the Laws of the State of New York, in the City of New York, this twenty-first day of November 1886. Witnesses to the Marriage: Bertha Moritz and Jacob Moritz. Signature of the person performing the Marriage Ceremony: H. Hebler, Clergyman. Residence, 173 E. 83 Str.

Reverse side of the certificate holds the following information:

1. Full name of Groom	John Vogelbach
2. Place of Residence	429 E. 81 Str
3. Age next Birthday	25 years
4. Blank line	
5. Occupation	Stair-builder
6. Place of Birth	Kussnach Switzerland
7. Father's Name	Anton Vogelbach
8. Mother's Maiden Name	Elisabeth Schnaebel
9. No. of Groom's Marriage	first
10. Full name of Bride	Fanny Moritz
11. Place of Residence	429 E. 81 Str
12. Age at next Birthday	21 years
13. Blank line	
14. Place of Birth	Winterthur Switzerland
15. Father's Name	Joseph Moritz
16. Mother's Maiden Name	Julie Eminirger
17. No. of Bride's Marriage	

N.B. At Nos. 4 and 13 state if Colored: If other races, specify what. The signatures below of Bride and Groom should be written out in full for the "given" and family names.
New York, November 21, 1886

We, the Groom and Bride named in the above Certificate, hereby Certify that the information given is correct, to the best of our knowledge and belief.
John Vogelbach, (Groom.) and Fanny Moritz (Bride.)
Signed in the presence of Bertha Moritz and Jacob Moritz.

The name and address of the church is not on the marriage certificate. Perhaps they were married in the church where Otto would later be baptized, Immanuel Lutheran at 88th St. and Lexington Ave. Both John and Fanny lived at the same address, "429 E. 81 Str." Kussnach, Switzerland is about 20 miles south of Zürich. Fanny said she was born in Winterthur, Switzerland. Otto's birth certificate gives her birthplace as Thalwil, Switzerland. The spelling of Eminirger is not clear on the certificate. It may be some other variant.

K – *John Vogelbach's Last Will and Testament – Transcription*[9]

KNOW ALL MEN BY THESE PRESENTS, that I, JOHN VOGELBACH, of Westbury, Nassau County, New York, hereby make, publish and declare this as and for my Last Will and Testament, hereby revoking any and all former wills by me at anytime heretofore made.

FIRST: I give and bequeath to my son OTTO A. VOGELBACH the sum of One Hundred ($100.) Dollars.

SECOND: I give and bequeath to my son JOSEPH A. VOGELBACH the sum of One Hundred ($100.) Dollars, and also all my tools.

THIRD: I give and bequeath to my son ADOLPH VOGELBACH the sum of One Hundred ($100.) Dollars.

FOURTH: I give and bequeath to my daughter OLGA JARGSDORF the sum of One Hundred ($100.) Dollars.

FIFTH: I give and bequeath to my daughter ROSELLA RITTER the sum of One Hundred ($100.) Dollars.

SIXTH: I give and bequeath to my daughter FANNY WILEY the sum of One Hundred ($100.) Dollars.

SEVENTH: All the rest, residue and remainder of my estate of whatever nature and wheresoever situate, I give, devise and bequeath to my daughter MARTHA VOGELBACH in appreciation of her devotion to me in caring for me and my household.

EIGHTH: I purposely leave nothing to my son LOUIS VOGELBACH from whom I have not heard for years and of whose whereabouts I am ignorant.

NINTH: I hereby direct and authorize my executor hereinafter named to sell my real estate at public and private sale, and to convey such estate by proper deeds of conveyance; and no purchaser shall be required to see to the application of the purchase money.

---

[9] Xerox copy of the original will is in the collection of the author.

TENTH: I hereby nominate and appoint the WHEATLEY HILLS NATIONAL BANK OF WESTBURY as the executor of this my Last Will and Testament and direct that no bond be required of it for the faithful performance of its duties hereunder.

IN WITNESS HEREOF, I have set my hand and seal this 31st day of January, One Thousand Nine Hundred and Thirty.

John Vogelbach (L.S.)

WITNESSES:
John J. Kvethen
Harry W. Baltazzi
Edward W. Staab

The foregoing instrument was subscribed by the above named Testator, JOHN VOGELBACH, on this 31st day of January, 1930, in our presence, and was at the same time published and declared by him to be his Last Will and Testament, and thereupon we, at his request and in his presence and in the presence of each other, did subscribed our names thereto as attesting witnesses, this attestation clause having first been read aloud to us in the presence of the said Testator.

John J. Kvethen	Residing at	343 Winthrop St., Westbury, NY
Harry W. Baltazzi		Westbury, NY
Edward W. Staab [10]		164 Butler St., Westbury, NY

---

[10] Peter Heidtmann identified Ed Staab as a board member of Wheatley Hills Bank who knew John Vogelbach very well. Ed Staab owned Staab's Hardware Store on Post Ave., Westbury.

L – Covington
Family Tree

Charles H COVINGTON
.. +Harriet COVINGTON
...... 2 [1] Rose May COVINGTON
.... +Louis VOGELBACH
.... +Harry VAN GEISEN
.... 3 Avery VAN GEISEN
.... +SOPHIE
.... 4 William H VAN GEISEN
.... 4 Avery F. VAN GEISEN
.... 4 Ruth E. VAN GEISEN
...... 2 George W. COVINGTON
.... +GERTRUDE
.... 3 Pearl COVINGTON
...... 2 Fred COVINGTON
.... +LULU
...... 2 Milo COVINGTON
.... +LILY
.... 3 Howard G. COVINGTON
.... +Mary Lou MAXWELL
.... 4 Margarette COVINGTON
...... 2 Manley COVINGTON
.... +ARLIE
.... 3 Roy COVINGTON

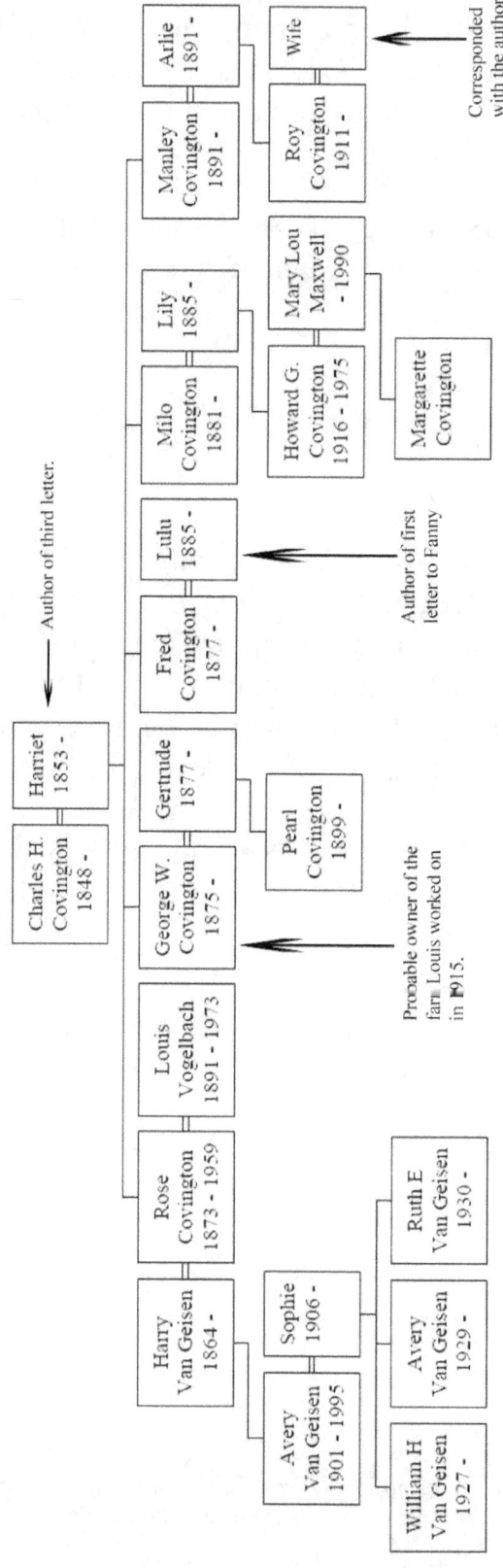

M – Marriage Certificate for Joseph Vogelbach and Florence Beyer

CERTIFICATE OF MARRIAGE

CHURCH OF OUR LADY OF ANGELS
7320 Fourth Avenue
Brooklyn, N.Y. 11209

✳   This is to Certify   ✳

That _Joseph Vogelbach_

and _Florence Beyer_

✳   Were Lawfully Married   ✳

on the ___12___ day of _October_ _1915_

According to the Rite of the Roman Catholic Church
and in conformity with the laws of the State of New York.

Rev. _Charles Reiley_

officiating, in the presence of _Julius Jargstoff_

and _Olga Vogelbach_ Witnesses,

as appears from the Marriage Register of this Church.

Dated _August 14 2000_

James E Devlin Pastor.

NO. 212 © D.P. MURPHY CO., INC., NY   11

---

[11] The parish secretary who provided this record to the author in 2000 made three transcript errors: Beyers, Reilly, and Jargstorff. She included a note apologizing for possible errors because she said she had trouble reading the handwriting, but she was kind enough to provide additional information she found in the parish register: Joseph Vogelbach resided at 639 Curtis Ave, Richmond Hill, Long Island. (Curtis Ave is now 124th Street.) Florence Beyers lived at 548 72nd Street, Brooklyn.

Bibliography

Books

Colletta, John P. *They Came in Ships: A Guide to Finding Your Immigrant Ancestor's Arrival Record.* Revised 3rd Edition. Orem, UT: Ancestry Publishing, an imprint of MyFamily.com, Inc., 2002

The Columbia Encyclopedia, Sixth Ed, online at www.bartleby.com

DeBartolo-Carmack, Sharon. *A Genealogist's Guide to Discovering Your Immigrant and Ethnic Ancestors.* Cincinnati OH: Betterway Books, an imprint of F&W Publications, 2000.

____. *Organizing Your Family History Search.* Cincinnati OH: Betterway Books, an imprint of F&W Publications, 1999.

____. *You Can Write Your Family History.* Salt Lake City UT: Ancestry Inc., 2003.

Glazier, Ira A. and P. William Filby, editors. *Germans to America: Lists of Passengers Arriving at U.S. Ports 1850-1897, Vol. 1-67.* Wilmington DE: Scholarly Resources, c1988-2002.

Hatcher, Patricia Law. *Producing a Quality Family History.* Salt Lake City UT: Ancestry Inc., 1996.

The Johns Hopkins Family Health Book. New York NY: HarperCollins Publishers, 1999.

Kempthorne, Charley. *For All Time: A Complete Guide to Writing Your Family History.* Portsmouth NH: Boynton/Cook Publishers (Heinemann), a subsidiary of Reed Elsevier, Inc., 1996.

McCutcheon, Marc. *Everyday Life in the 1800's: a Guide for Writers.* Cincinnati OH: Writer's Digest Books, 2001.

Mills, Elizabeth Shown. *Evidence! Citation and Analysis for the Family Historian.* Balt. MD: Genealogical Pub. Co., 1997

Panchyk, Richard. *A History of Westbury, LI,* The History Press, 2007. (available on Google Books)

Szucs, Loretto Dennis. *They Became Americans: Finding Naturalization Records and Ethnic Origins.* Salt Lake City UT: Ancestry Inc., 1998.

Tepper, Michael. *American Passenger Arrival Records.* Baltimore, MD: Genealogical Publishing Co., Inc., 1993.

Databases consulted and Records Repositories used:

1880-1925 Manhattan, Queens, and Brooklyn Directories. Variously available on microfilm at the 42nd Street Library, New York City, on Family History Library microfilms, and online at www.Ancestry.com

1892, 1905, 1915, 1925 New York State Censuses, New York, Kings, and Queens Counties [Family History Library microfilms]

1900, 1910, 1920, and 1930 United States Federal Censuses [databases on-line at Ancestry.com]. Original data: United States of America, Bureau of the Census. Washington, D.C.: National Archives and Records Administration. (1900: T623, 1854 rolls), (1910: T624, 1,178 rolls), (1920: T625, 2,076 rolls), (1930: T626, 2,667 rolls).

1939 Binghamton City Directory [database on-line at Ancestry.com]

Green-Wood Cemetery Records, 500 25th Street, Brooklyn NY 11232-1317 [and online at www.green-wood.com]

National Archives and Records Administration, Northeast Region, New York City, 201 Varick Street, 12th Floor, New York, NY 10014.

New Jersey State Archives, Department of State, PO Box 307, 225 West State Street, Trenton, NJ 08625-0307

NYC Department of Records and Information Services, Vital Records Archives Division, 31 Chambers St., New York, NY.

New York State Department of Health, Certification Unit, Vital Records Section, P.O. Box 2602, Albany, NY 12220-2606

Connecticut Death Index [database online at www.Ancestry.com]

NYS Bridge Authority History, http://www.nysba.state.ny.us/Index.html

The New York Times Archive 1851-1980. [Online access through New York Times Select subscription]

NYC's Transit Museum [online at http://www.transitmuseumeducation.org/trc/background]

Parish Registry of Our Lady of Angels RC Church, 7320 Fourth Avenue, Brooklyn NY 11209.

Parish Registry of St. Paul's Lutheran Church, 120 Herriman Ave., Jamaica, NY [currently at 127-27 102nd Street]

Parish Registry of German Evangelical Lutheran Immanuel Church, East 88th and Lexington Ave, New York, NY.

Friends Cemetery Records, 550 Post Ave, Westbury NY.

New York Passenger Lists, 1820-1957 [database on-line at Ancestry.com]. Original data: *Passenger Lists of Vessels Arriving at New York, New York, 1820-1897*; (National Archives Microfilm Publication M237, 675 rolls); Records of the U.S. Customs Service, Record Group 36; National Archives, Washington, D.C. and *Passenger and Crew Lists of Vessels Arriving at New York, New York, 1897-1957*; (National Archives Microfilm Publication T715, 8892 rolls); Records of the Immigration and Naturalization Service; National Archives, Washington, D.C.

Passenger and Immigration Lists Index, 1500s-1900s, Gale Research. [database on-line at Ancestry.com]. Provo, UT, USA: The Generations Network, Inc., 2006. Original data: Filby, P. William, ed.. *Passenger and Immigration Lists Index, 1500s-1900s.* Farmington Hills, MI, USA: Gale Research, 2006.

Passenger Lists of Vessels Arriving at New York, New York, 1820-1897; (National Archives Microfilm Publication M237, 675 rolls); Records of the U.S. Customs Service, Record Group 36; National Archives, Washington, D.C.

Registrar, Pilgrim Psychiatric Center, L. I. State Hospital Archives, 998 Crooked Hill Rd, West Brentwood, NY 11717-1087

Social Security Death Index [database on-line at Ancestry.com], Provo, UT, USA: The Generations Network, Inc., 2007. Original data drawn from Social Security Administration, *Social Security Death Index*, Master File.

Swiss Archives: Ansässenverzeichnis von Thalwil (E III 121.19) and Niedergelassenenverzeichnis of Veltheim (1835-1883).

Broome County Library Obituary Collection, 185 Court Street, Binghamton, NY 13901.

Chenango Valley Cemetery Records, 120 Nowlan Road, Binghamton, NY 13901.

World War I Draft Registration Cards, 1917-1918 [database on-line at Ancestry.com]. Original data: United States, Selective Service System. *World War I Selective Service System Draft Registration Cards, 1917-1918.* Washington, D.C.: National Archives and Records Administration. M1509, 4,582 rolls.

U.S. Phone and Address Directories, 1993-2002 [database on-line at Ancestry.com].

U.S. World War II Army Enlistment Records, 1938-1946 [database on-line at Ancestry.com]. Original data: *Electronic Army Serial Number Merged File, 1938-1946*; World War II Army Enlistment Records; Records of the National Archives and Records Administration, Record Group 64; National Archives at College Park, College Park, MD.

U.S. World War II Draft Registration Cards, 1942 [database on-line at Ancestry.com]. Original data: United States, Selective Service System. *Selective Service Registration Cards, World War II: Fourth Registration.* National Archives and Records Administration Branch locations: National Archives and Records Administration Region Branches.

Miscellaneous

E-mails, letters, and telephone conversations with John Black, Veronica Black, Virginia Black, Grace Doheny, Eileen Greenlees, Elizabeth Gundlach, Peter Heidtmann, Gretchen Horwath, Olga Hughes, Beverly Hutchinson, Joan Martin, Ruth Bush, Barbara Roebuck, Anne Schuessler, Ronald Vogelbach, Joseph Wylie, and especially Charles Oscar Roebuck.

Vogelbach Family Tree, hand-drawn by Charles Oscar Roebuck, PO Box 35, Thompson Ridge NY in 1987, titled "VOGELBACH – A Swiss who served with Napoleon in the Russian campaign for seven years."

Helliesen Family Tree, hand drawn by Harold Helliesen. The original is in the possession of Linda Helliesen Miller, 2189 Blossomwood Drive, Oviedo FL 32765.

Memorial Cards for Frank Buhse, Jeanne Buhse, John Martin, Florence E. Vogelbach, Joseph Vogelbach.

Index

This index lists all the people and places mentioned in this book. Variant spellings for names have been conflated (merged) into single entries for the reader's convenience. Page numbers in **bold** refer to the primary page(s) for an individual. Page numbers in *italics* refer to photographs or illustrations.

Women are listed under their maiden name and all married names. Individuals with unknown surnames are at the beginning of the index.

With regard to women's married and maiden names, *See* references go from the married name to the maiden name. Women's married names are in [ ]; their maiden names are in ( ).

Towns and counties are listed under the state or country in which they are located.

Major categories include Addresses, Censuses, Certificates, Churches, Illnesses and diseases, Occupations and Hobbies, Surnames, and Towns and Cities.

If there are several identical male given names under one surname, an attempt has been made, for the convenience of the reader, to identify unique individuals either by birthday, mother's name, or by some other identifier within parentheses ( ).

Abbreviations: RC (Roman Catholic), NYC (New York, NY), and US Post Office codes for states in the USA.